MW01629164

SEISMOSIS

Seismosis * 1913 press: www.1913press.org

design: floating media * cover art: stackhouse
* cover design: ben doyle *
printed in the united states of america * the oldest country in the world
* first edition *
 * ISBN 0-9779351-0-8
* typefaces from the year 1913: gil sans & nicholas cochin *
this publication is supported in generous part by grants & labor from individuals, whose dedication to innovative work made this project possible

1913
Press

www.1913press.org

S E I S M O S I S

text:
John Keene

|

drawing:
Christopher Stackhouse

1913
Press

www.1913press.org

John extends many thanks to Jeffrey Renard Allen, Kevin Bell, Tisa Bryant,
Krista Franklin, Shannon Gibney, Eric Hamel, Duriel Harris, Reggie Harris, Paul Laster,
Toni Asante Lightfoot, Nate Mackey, Dave Moore, Mendi Lewis Obadike,
all my colleagues and students at Northwestern University,
all who invited us to read from this work and all who published early versions of it,
Rory Golden and everyone at the Center for Book Arts,
the Fund for Poetry and the New Jersey State Council on the Arts,
Veronica Corpuz, who first proposed it,
our wonderful publisher, Sandra Miller, and designer Jonathan Thirkield,
and of course, to Christopher Stackhouse,
without whom this wouldn't have been possible.

Chris thanks Dorothy White, Stan Lewis, Ronnie Corpuz,
The Center For Book Arts, Rory Golden, Cave Canem,
The New York Foundation for The Arts, Greg Coates,
Sandra Miller, Jonathan Thirkield, David Lantow,
The Kivland Family, Sipio Small, Catherine Lewis, Yael Sadan,
Michael Trotman, Alisoun Meehan, Jamie Gray, John Keene,
Skip, Carol, Zane, and Kelly.
Marks of adoration and some kind of love to you all.

for Curtis Allen

for Nailah and Satya

SEISMOSIS

TEXTS

DRAWINGS*

**from* Perpendicular Series

FOREWORD

Ed Roberson

Seismosis is an astounding collaboration—a conversation between a visual and a verbal artist, a communication between friends. The reader becomes involved in this thoughtful interplay between two art forms—both of which ask us what we see before our field of observation settles or finalizes into an object or its word.

We've noticed artists before, in both forms, just before touching the pencil to the page, move the instrument above the surface toward some settlement: where to start? & whatever is the poem or drawing going to be? We feel the noise and the possibilities of pre-conception in exchange here. This book attempts to map the territory of those moments: Stackhouse with his seismographic writing of that visual noise, Keene with his de-systematized syntax of space.

And prior to this conversation, Keene also drew and Stackhouse also wrote. Likewise, the different lives of each art form—in that selfsame moment of creating the page—seem to lift out of their respective forms in reaching to the other. Here, the artist challenges the writer with *'the lines of drawing that written language is, without the discipline of its given system.'* Here, the writer challenges the artist to '*an elemental response code*' to share the other's emotional impulses. Challenges of drawing to write and of writing to draw free of letter.

Once this reach-across is established, the more daring and intimate exchanges can begin: What is drawing's *word* for "self"? What is the placement, the location of a sentiment's *color*? These questions do not become simple explorations of synesthesia, but exist rather as deeply philosophical and psychological tests of experience and perception.

On first perusal, this book could appear to be the notes of an innovative lecture; it isn't. *Seismosis* is the complete text for the course, replete with illustrations, examples, graphs, exercises, and tests. This isn't a gut course; it takes guts—and brains, and eyes, and....

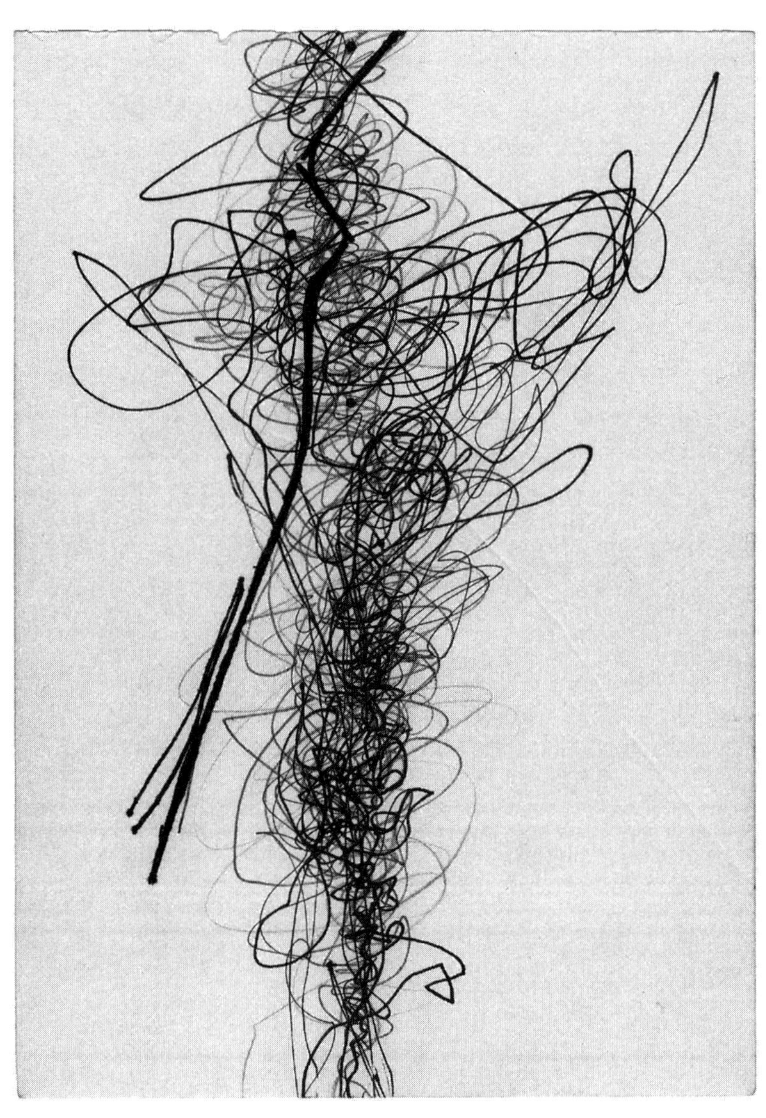

In the mark event, you enter your signature.

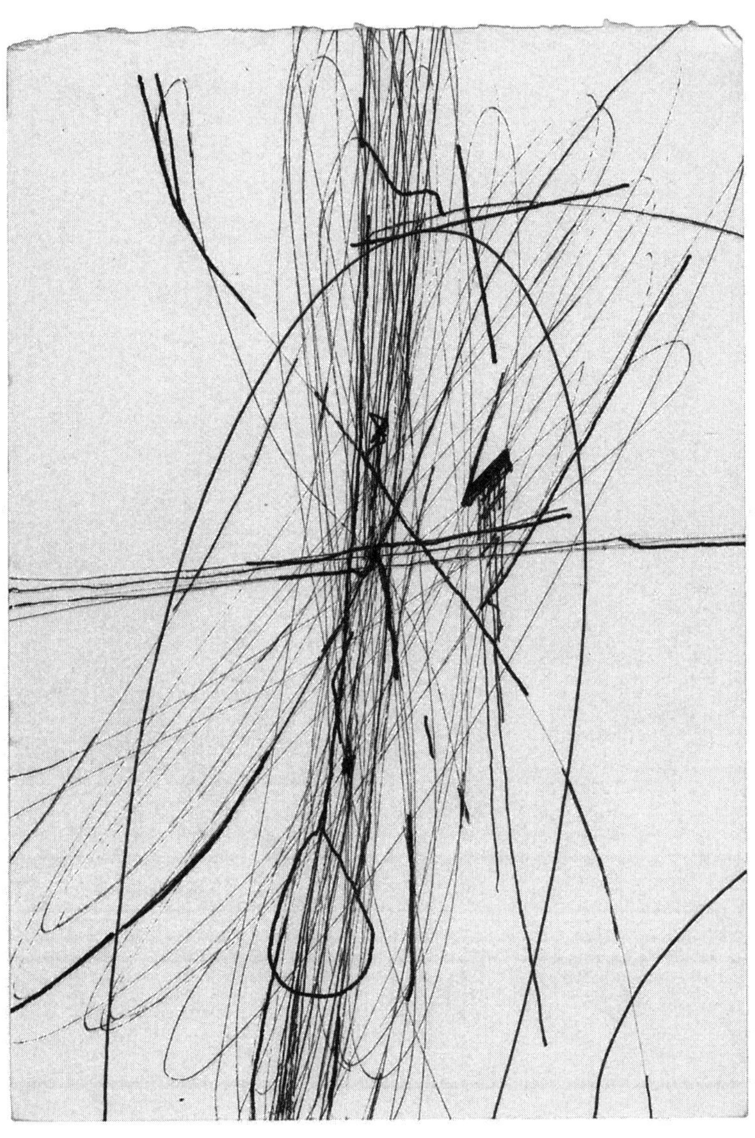

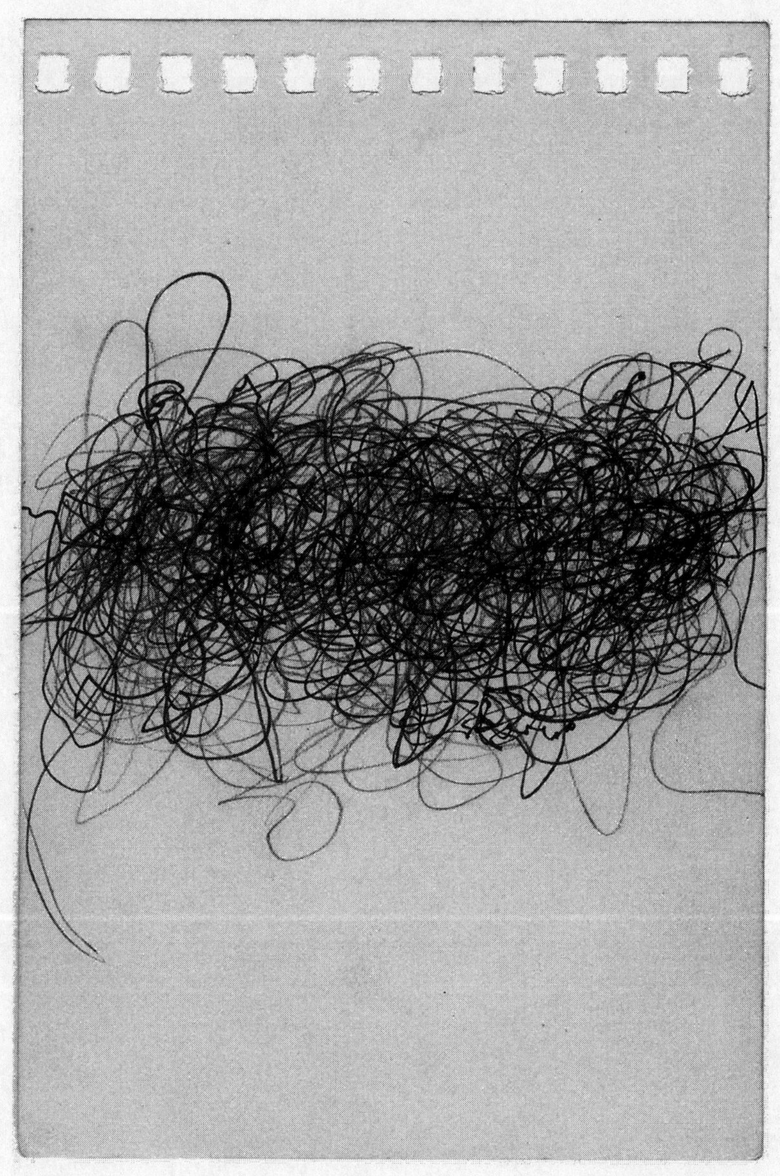

CONDENSATION I

"For a long time I was drawing regularly. I've drawn since I was small, even before I uttered a word or penned my own name. My chief motivation for drawing is, I guess, what it is for those who have no aims beyond self-expression. It's an intimate act, my main means of getting what's inside me or outside me down, on a page, it's a refuge, an act of love. I guess you could say I've always loved to draw, to create in images worlds I haven't yet seen or cannot live or experience, except through the drawings. But I ceased for a little while, stopped drawing regularly, and yet I continued to and sometimes still do inhabit those secret regions that I created with pencil strokes or the tip of a pen, to the detriment, some friends and loved ones have claimed, of real-world experiences and relationships. Those close to me have said things like perhaps I wasn't living enough in the present, in the now, in and for today. Perhaps I was forestalling my current reality for some fantasy I'd realized only in my drawings. It was real there but nowhere else, sort of like my interiority exteriorized, the place where the real truths of my life and experiences, my existence, inhere."

To resort to other expressive methods, other ways of deriving the called thing, drawing. Without you. Through color the key, the eyes the harmonies, the soul palette with its innumerable stirrings. Can it be trapped as a figure, the perceptual color. Is it clear where the color space lies, where string and range begin. Without you, whether the fingers that play are representable, the fingers that say: artist. One layer beside another, differentiable, where tendency is evident, one key or another, the graphic that enfolds, withholds. From closing to stitching. Vibrations as color. Touching drawing. Compact or not compact, call things soul, represent them as differentiable. Where it is clearest is lyrical, where it passes through itself as connections, figures mass. Without you, the other ways, through methods tying the spectrum to what stays, what plays beneath the other layers, untying the last one. Without keys or harmonies. And where would it be, without you?

FIELD

The augured grid: whose traces: these gradient strings replay: an object in field: to store parameters: need or nothing less: in reticule the radiant net: emerges: you object to: rigid, the local gray: paths you drive down: gradually perceive the performance: and all its configurations: displacement from yesterday and ideal: as it settles here: delay setting in, permutations: of line: your plasticity or mind: registers lapping and skipping: through what comes back: crops up: ghost paths: upon a graded field: multiple roads you navigate: as one who tries setting: to know through: invisible creeps in: to you as geometric directives: but I sought that: you say, displacement of grids: I heard as hollows: fields bearing the idea: of incident sound, found: sentiment, of correspondent forms: or nearness: what I face: or fear feeling having to: erotics of touch: that much or nothing less: in the net you field: objects instead, replacing hierarchy: with a theory of traces: two isomorphic spaces possess: a diverse set of interpreters.

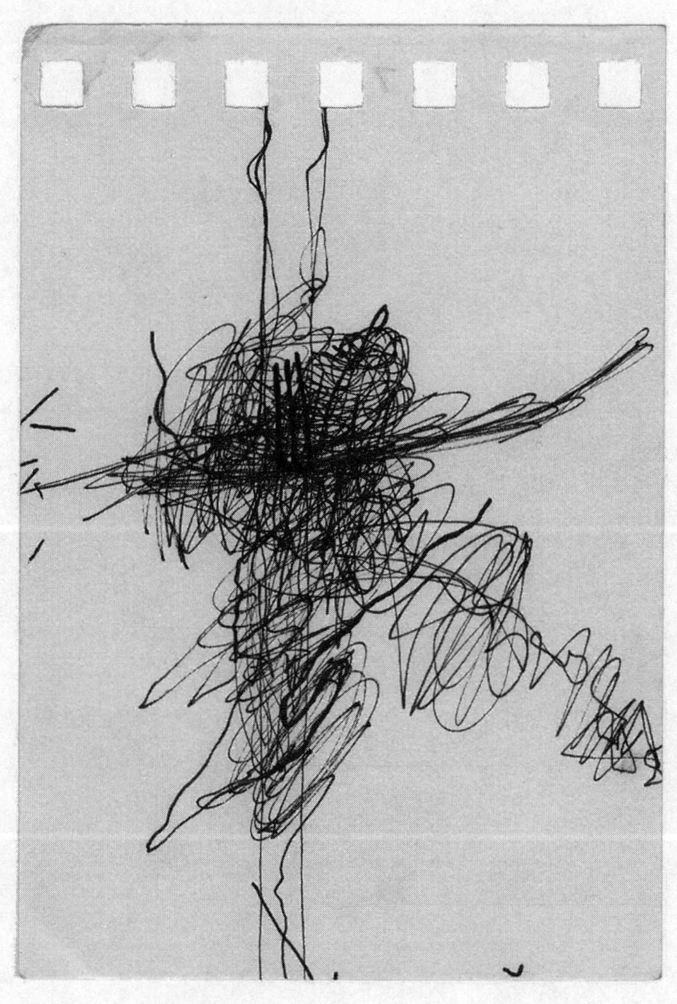

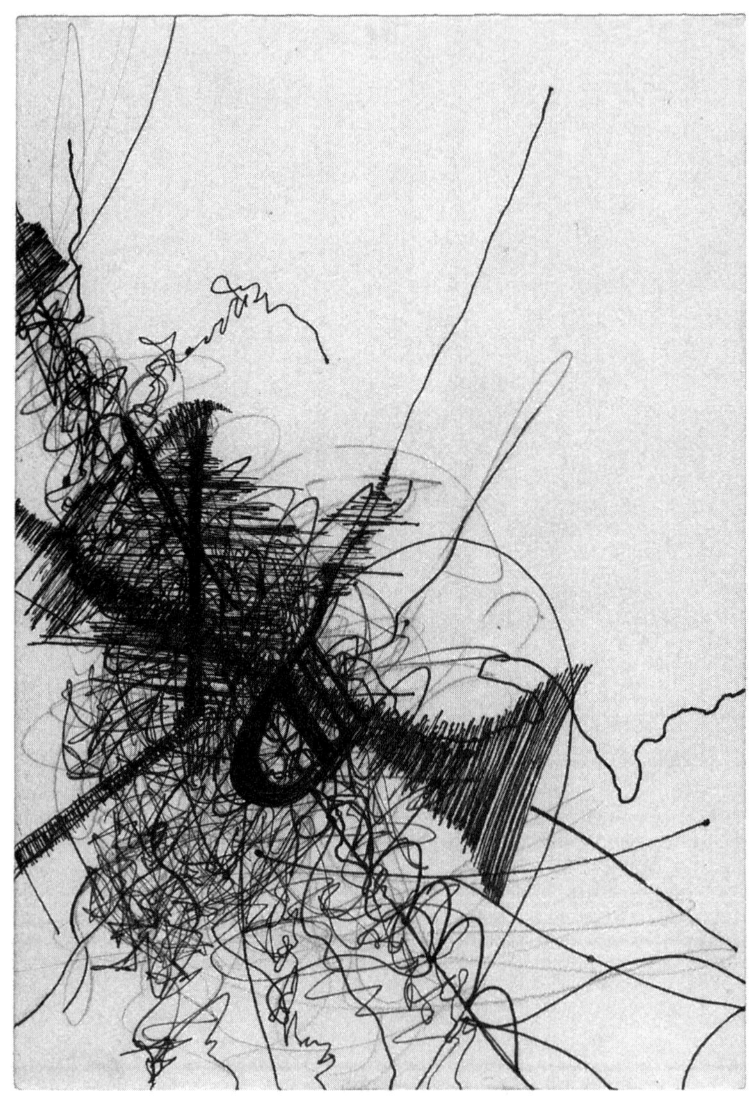

J: aura, or the lyrical-contemplative tendency
S: beyond its window, its shadow I am recoding
J: vestiges of instance, the instant
S: every stage and its ensemble, symbolic fractures
J: law the axion drives through into line
S: fractious or insistent rhythm
J: (intenting)
S: links or break
J: aura, mytho-kinetic dynamics
S: finding (play) or mining unseamed
J: act in matrix
S: transaction—what emerges from the unseen streaming into
J: (out of) margins
S: leaking contact (origins)
J: center or plane
S: what duels or chords through transition, what emanates
J: unveils, dwelling in surplus
S: (reveals)
J: what derives through line, coupling
S: in private figures
J: sorting, interior cutting (I)
S: aura, complex hiding and lapping
J: shadow geometries, synthetic origins

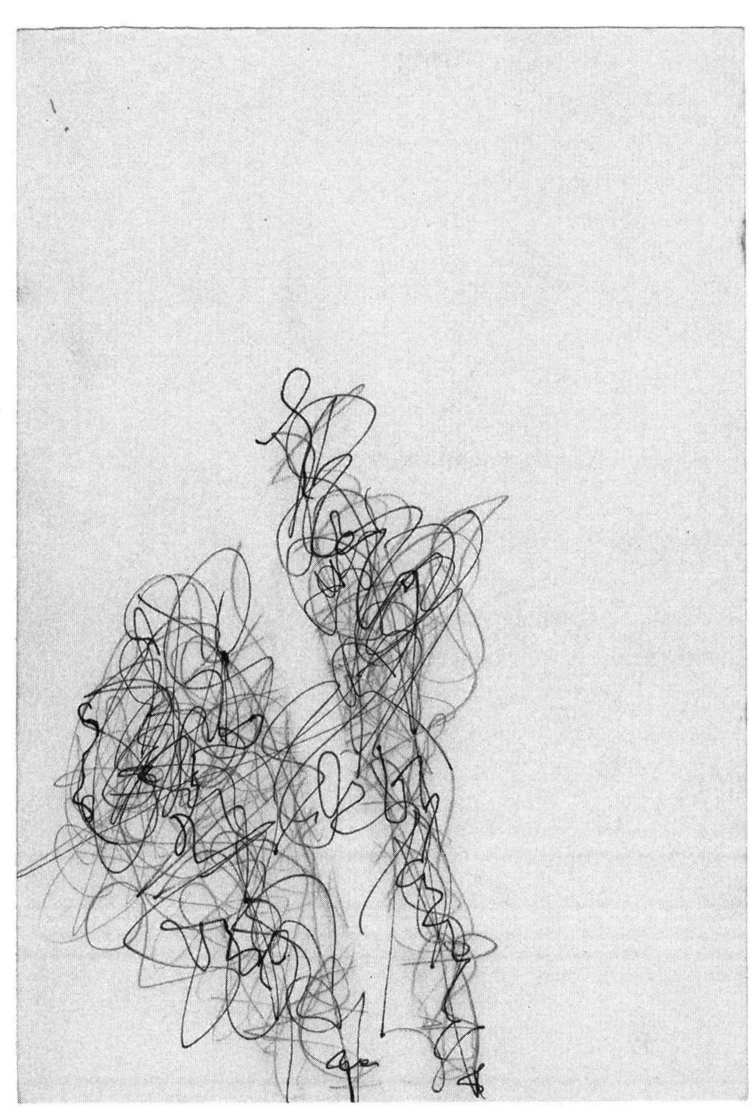

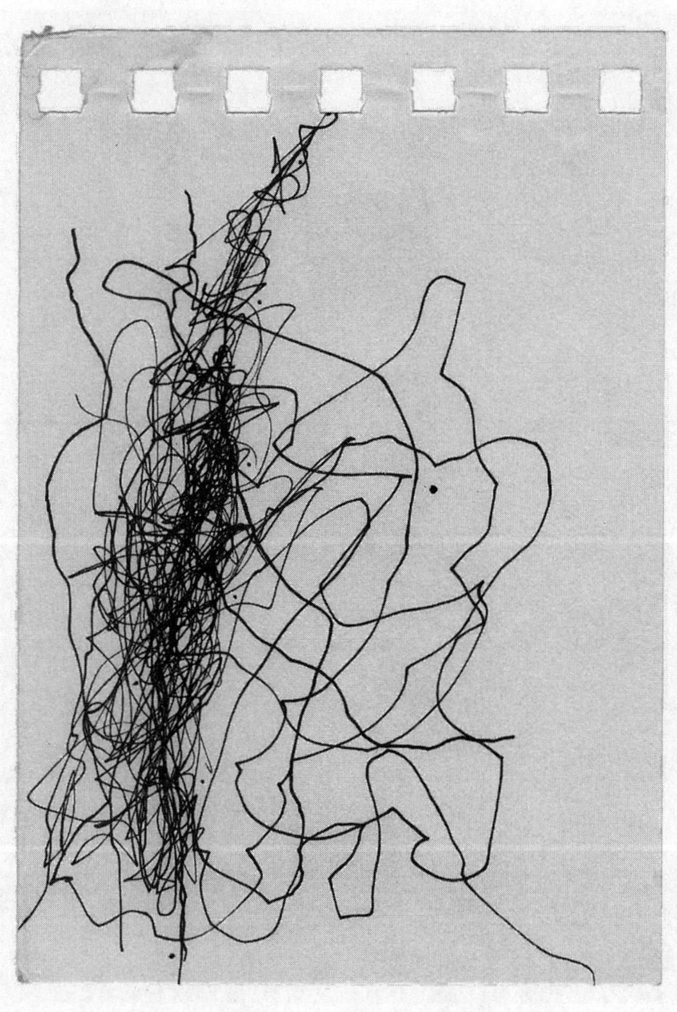

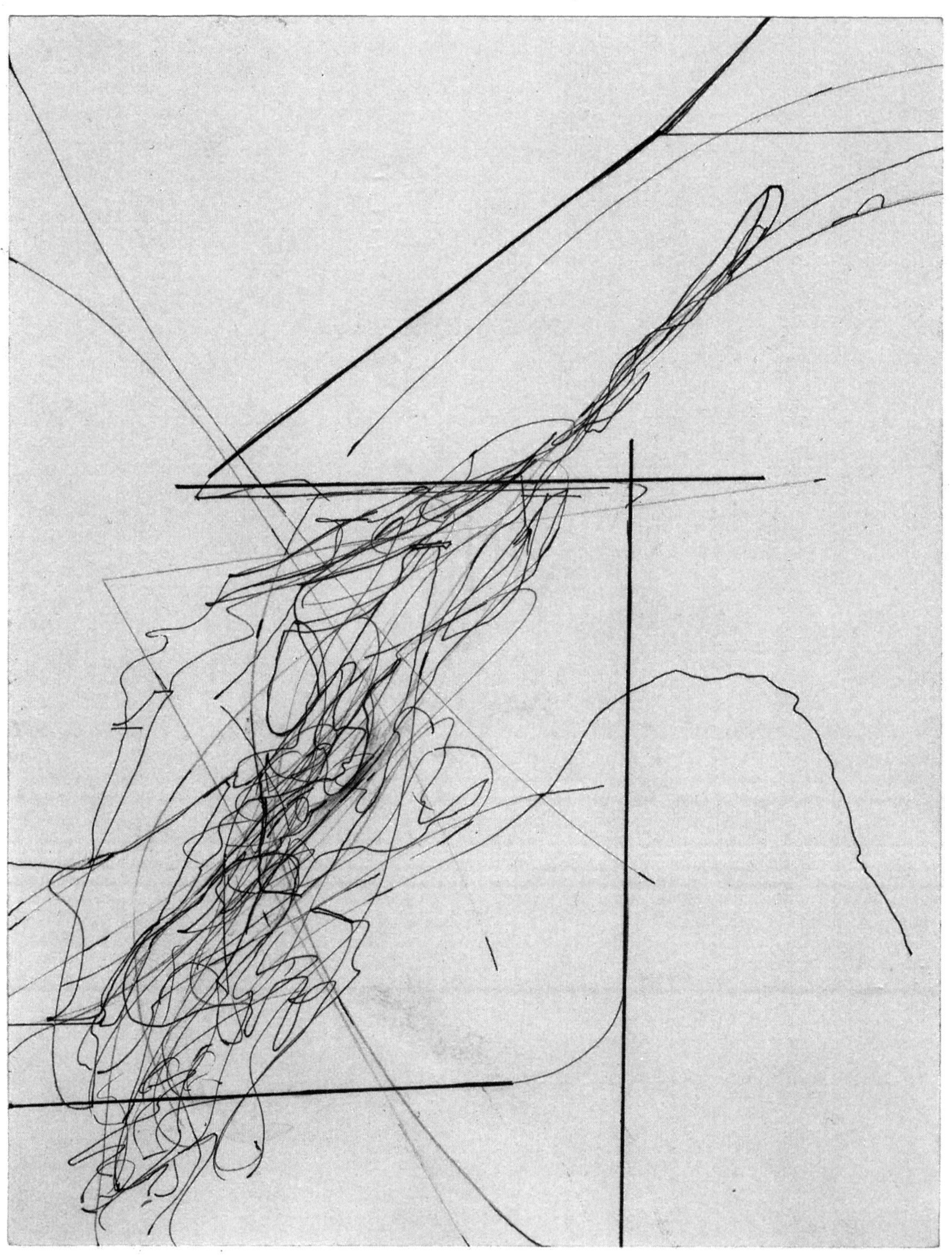

With respect to true north, each angle.
With respect to apparent position, event horizon.
Along the margins you sketch in small markers, magnetic scores
by which to pursue
the zero discourse.
Degree is lost in a clockwise fashion.
With respect to condition, describe the means by
which each concept aims to affect representation.
Via psychological seiche and external angles.

From the center, the counter of the image horizon cannot suffice.
Counterbalanced, not
metonymic. With respect to degree, distance.
With respect to correspondence, linkage.
The exact
position of your objects never given.
At the juncture of numerous conceptual planes.

Only depiction, distance and the distinct correlation between your lines and their
erasure.
Between
them, mythic refraction.
With respect to understanding, aesthetic pressure.
After the thought
corresponding to little but repetition itself, and increasing in a clockwise fashion.
With respect
to result, no values are refuted.

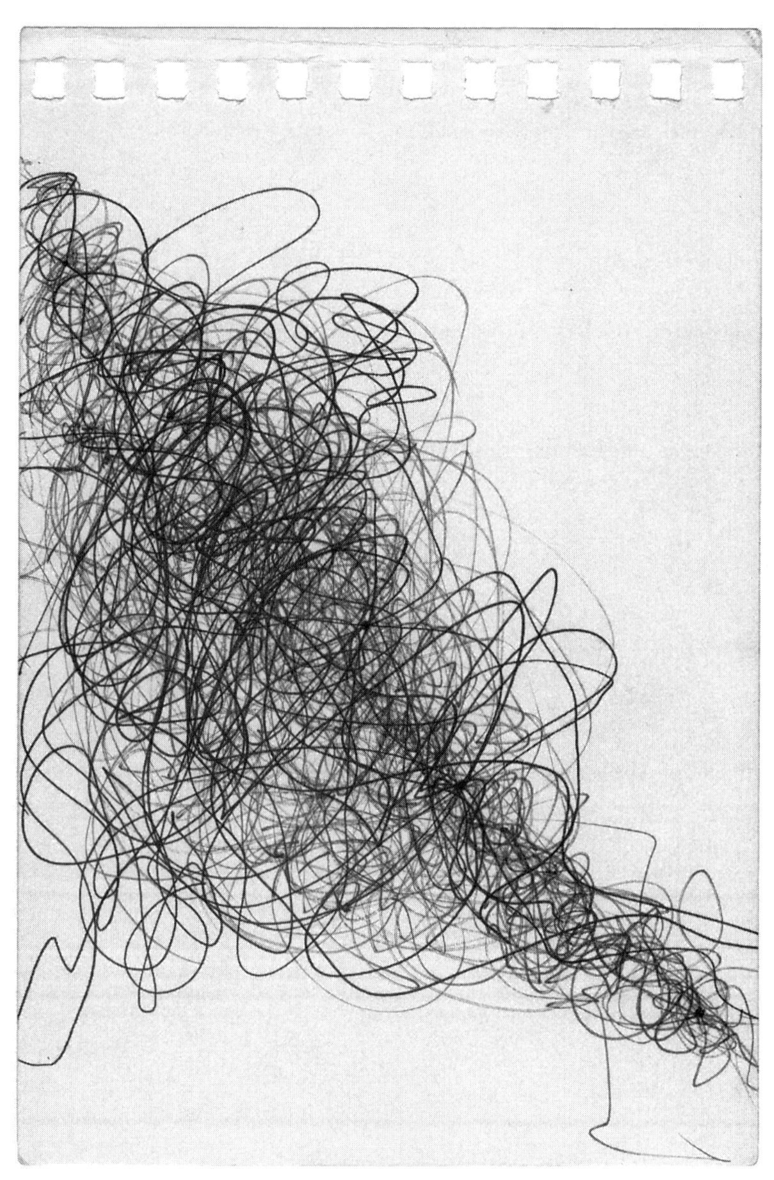

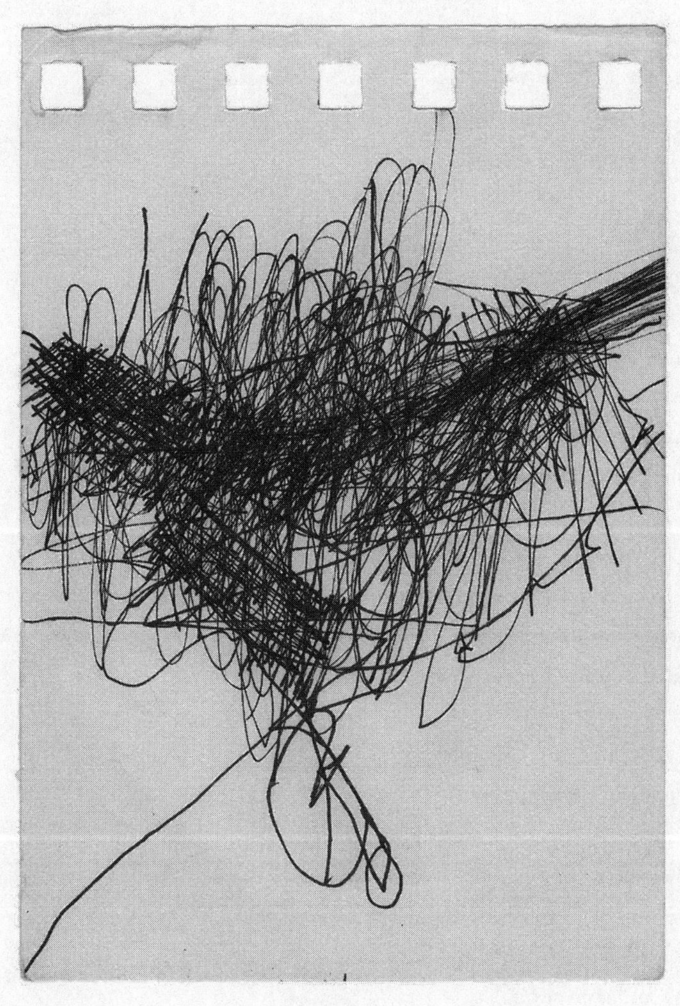

AFTER C (4): EVENT LOCATION

Emerging, through shadings...he tries
to ferment possibilities and mind them—
balance surface textures, shadow spaces
distilling what lies there. His urges

begin in listening to viewing...he tries
to eke out depth in extemporaneity,
simultaneous movements to figure and throw
where imagination stations then lets go.

For and through him, owing and owning
this impulse to compose, to cop some
movement and push himself into
each visual challenge. Conditional,

not photographic, yet freeing up what confines
in most of us encompassing depth and analysis.
Modeling an economy harder and more
revelatory, all ground and marks,

stretching himself to a level of being gone
at the moment of gut and presentation.
As in an incipient space, the search for an approach
to deconstruct his erasure. Scribbling

being, reading and pursuing each approximate tale,
tipped by collective and conceptual
implications. Always an edge towards true being,
mingling all expression, becoming anew.

visible	topoi	echoing	spiral	delay
density	sets	merge	coupling	symmetries
rapturous	boundary	graphing	subjective	technique
interior	threading	transitory	labyrinthine	cartography
faultline	rhythm	signals	lyric	plenitude

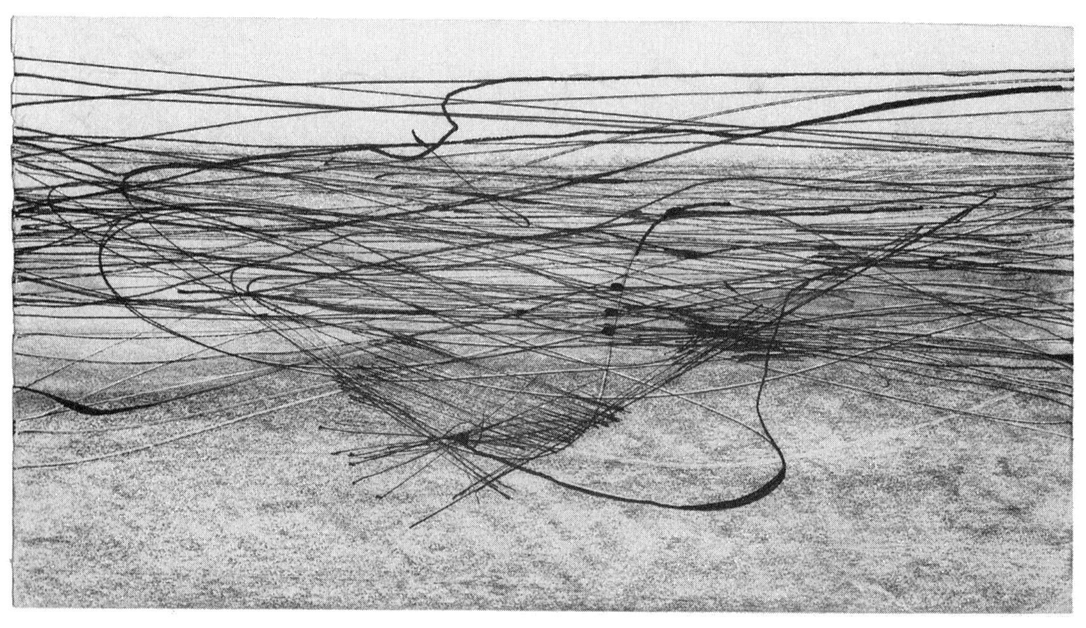

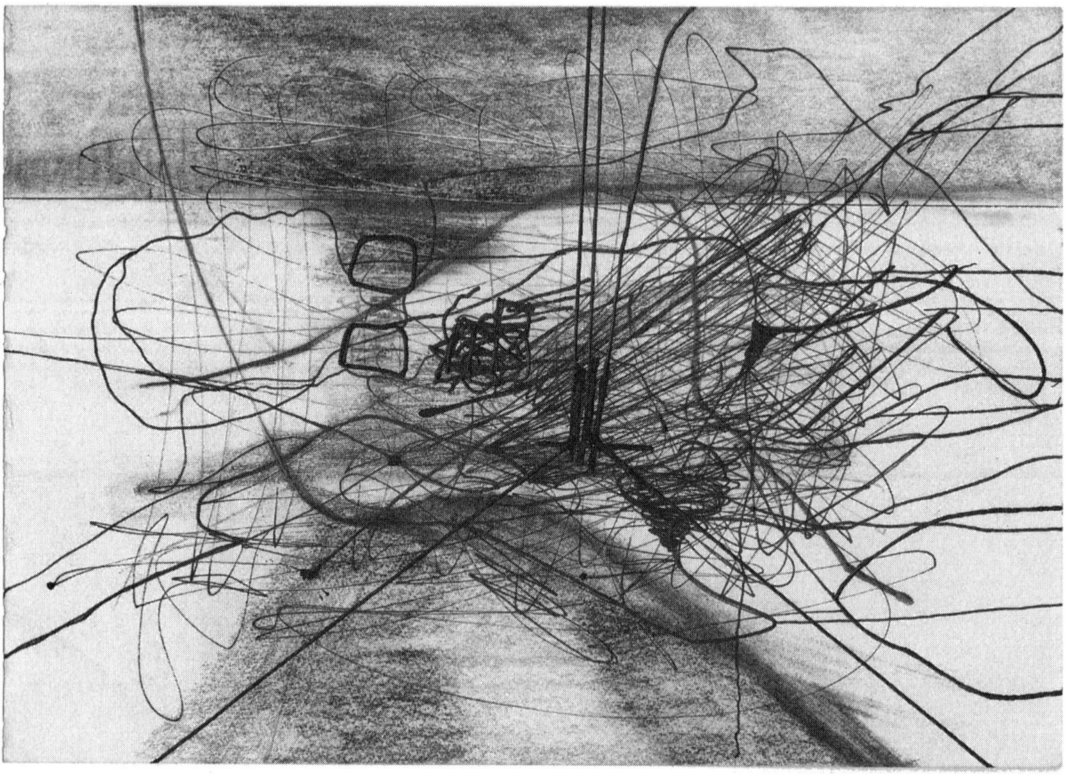

Self, black self, is there another label?*

*Raised to itself as global agent, figure and ground impel representation.

*Does selving assign or resignify?

*Does it overlap merely as configuration of lines or psychosexual momenta?

*In the mark, how does one identify authenticity or its inverse?

*Subjects arise or arrive, geometric in perspective, layer in sleeves into which identity presses.

*Subjectivity: or is there another label?

*In the selving, in a variety of mathematical applications, a shearing into abstract models yet visual logic retains the inner contours' pictographic properties.

*Self, black self, is there differentiation?

*A rivening in which superposition remaps loosely upon the other.

*Preconceptualizations arise on each differentiable map.

*The inverse of one self overlapping another.

*In nature, expression, or there is an Other?

*In the image, planar space disrupts the placement through which the selving transforms.

*Self, label the global versus the local in each dialogic vector.

*To precisely describe all configurations, positionalities and momenta, he draws the black images to shore up these parameters.

*In the end, refuse signature.

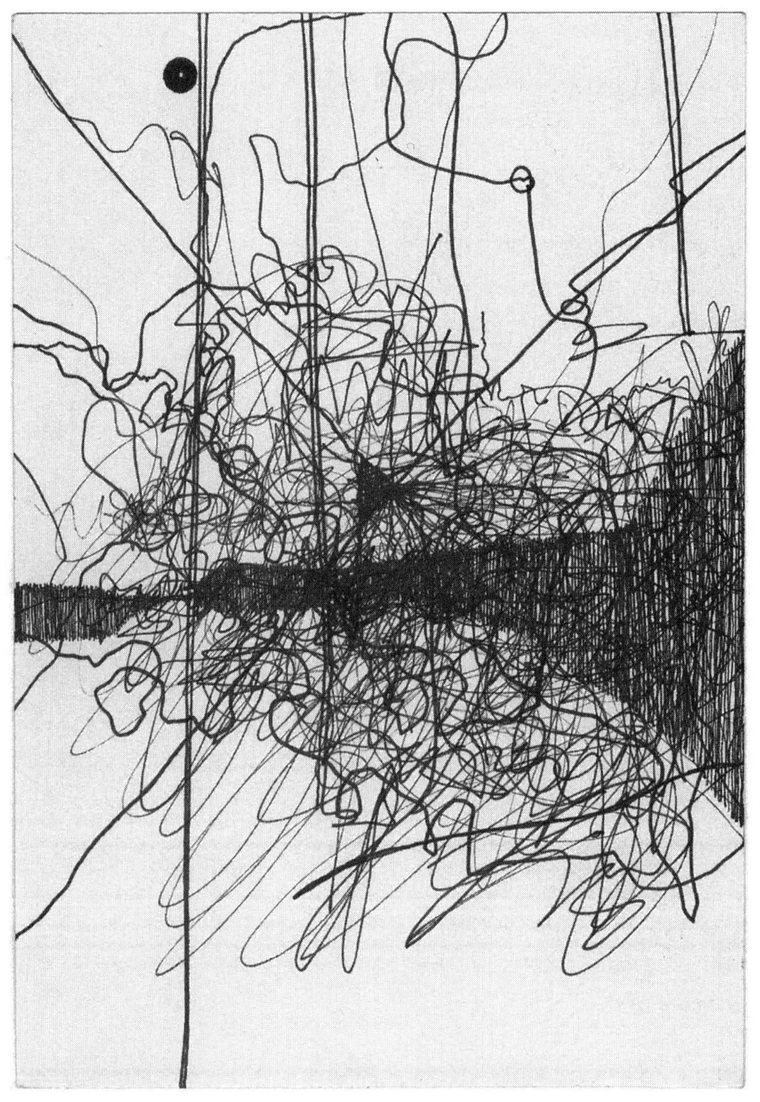

beneath your iris or fundamental variable
beneath your world and its referent response
I lift it however I peer in, entering
current and extension
reminded of drafts I
have seen, a tension of spiral, extending
sensation into line tone time and rhythm
mark architecture
attentive to the physical conversation
I am behind an oscillating
psychic screen
the scene of the act,
envisioning beauty and its planar articulation
I am in your chamber cinema
below root imaginary, a dialogue exposed
in which becoming will
breathe, think, live, work, cry, crap, die
but track free play of dreams
and distill them
to their furthest extremes as dreams and symbolic expression
pairing
contraries on which they lie
still within
condition, how tactile relevance holds system and
ethic
within cohesion, the conversation
of finger and iris physicality or deflection
straight but close, from distance
and reflective vantage
soul seethes and shifts
the improvisatory pleasure
of making
drawing seeds
recedes

METAPHYSICS

As in Driskell, the small metaphorical forms, ecstatic without boundary.

Intensified and shadowed signs graphed as a skein of reveries in a world around them.

One means identity's landscape, concise or layered.

One means forms deduced from epic traces, the topoi of possible degrees of accuracy.

Connection within disconnection.

As in Gilliam, outlined forms of landscape or escape which depart from calligraphic strategy.

Expansive, translated from large forms, now refractive and condensed, now grown immense and eruptive.

One means without boundaries.

To arrange the signs for which the gestures align in interpretive structures.

As in White, where an artist elects and then exaggerates the influences of a metaphysics, signifying message or passage as pure gesture or space.

One means a freedom from strategy, how the image selects itself as the means of representing the translation of forms.

One means other than verisimilitude: where identity ruptures.

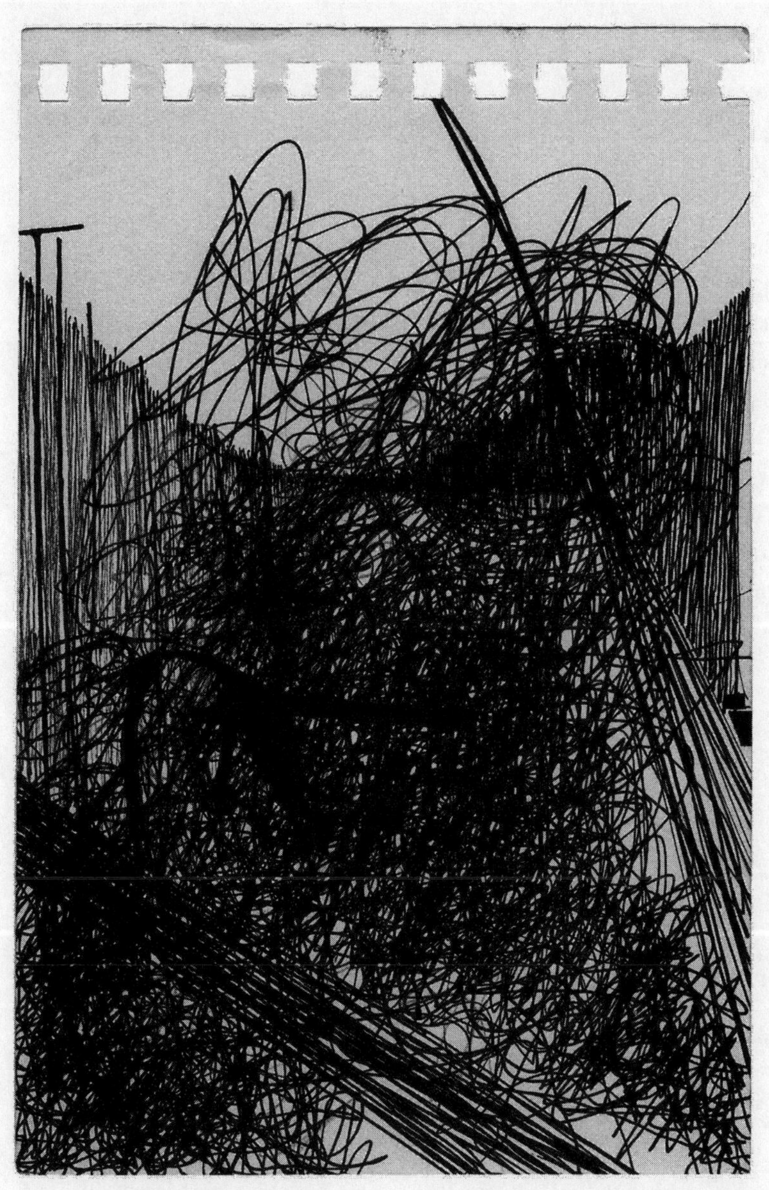

INDEX

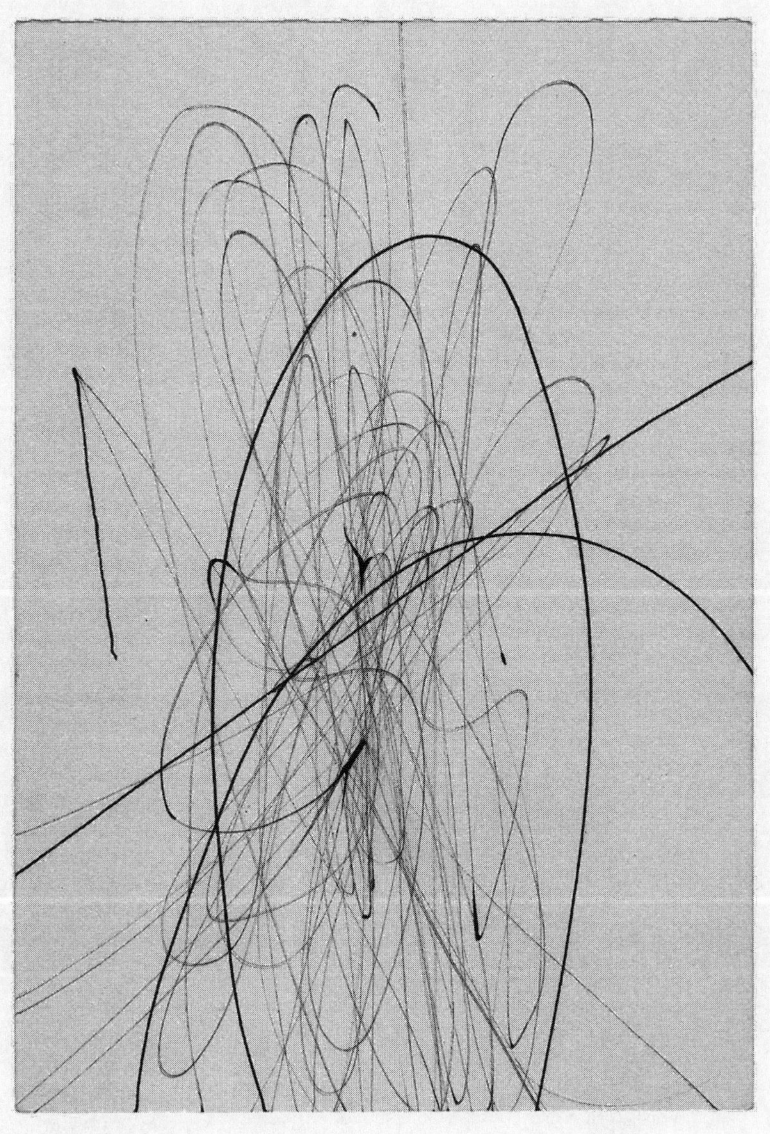

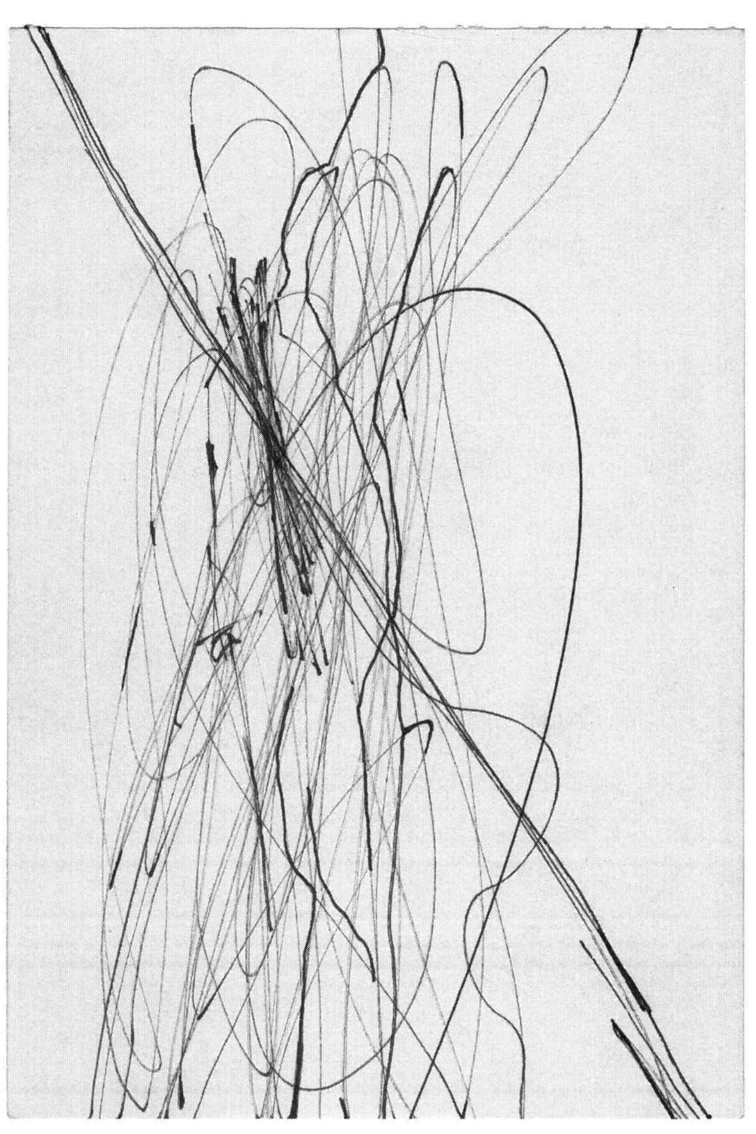

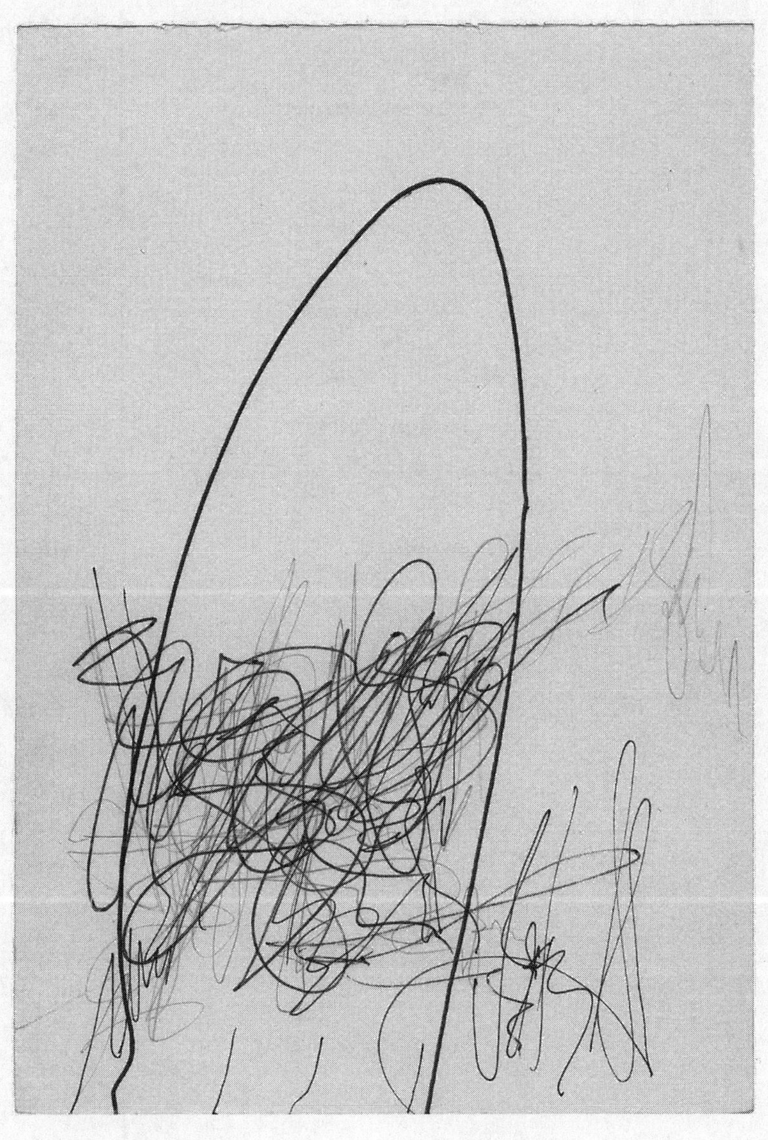

“between jointness”
“and surface”
“not externally driven”
“prior rhythms”

“towards disunity”
“forms”
“continuous”
“in rigor”

“where faults settle”
“forcing thought through”
“the disparate hand”
“visions loosed”
“lost and searching”

“oneiric studies”
“diagonals rain”
“in a field”
“or its mirror”

“not austere”
“touching”
“frames weave”
“cleaving the closeness”

“by eye”
“spinning unities”
“in sense”
“threading differs”
“according to acts or axis”
“intensities”

“at termini”
“a facility”
“method painting”
“exhilaration”

“differing”
“axes”
“order”
“frame”

“austere”
“intensities”
“settle”
“closer”

“eyes”
“touch”
“rigorous”
“method”
“fields”

“mirrors”
“pointing”
“image”
“surfaces”

“continuous”
“senses”
“spin”
“diagonals”

“hand”
“searching”
“form”
“joining”
“nonlinear”
“unity”

“disparate”
“phrases”
“weaving”
“rain”

if p then perception

reducing surface physical responses

fragments hinge

cartographies float against finality

clouding layers

on paper slope light-intensity and action

map compositional signal levels

serpentine patterns trap

as momenta charts of identity

if conception *then p*

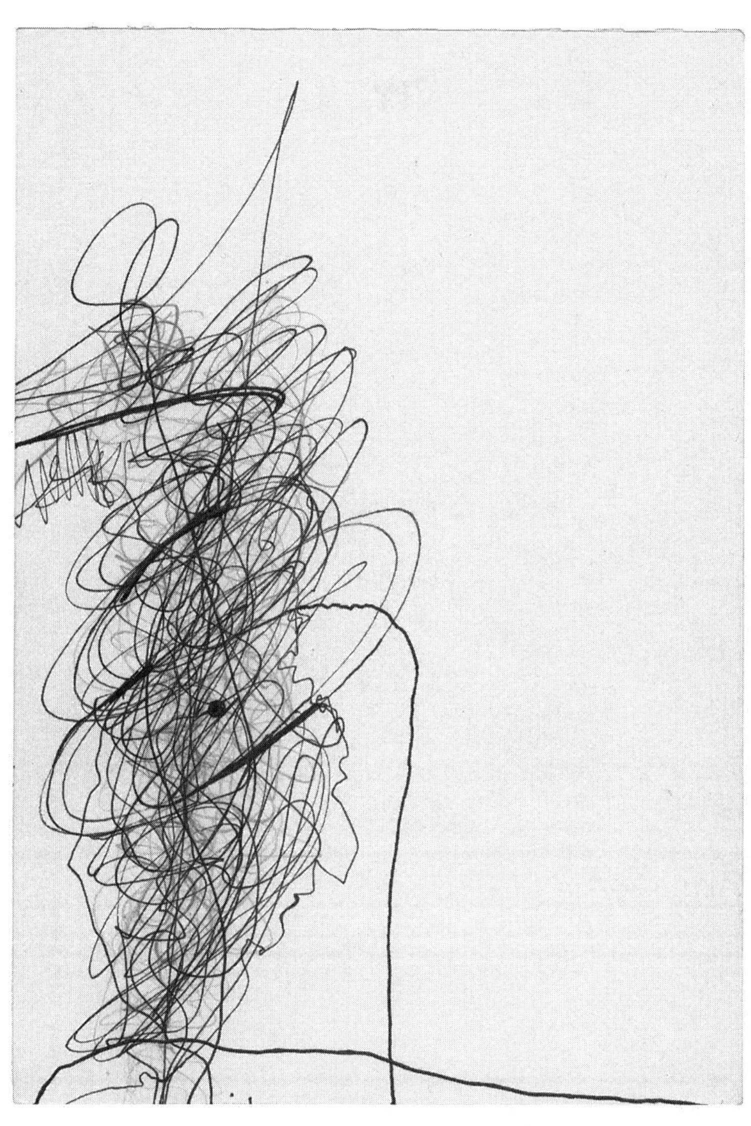

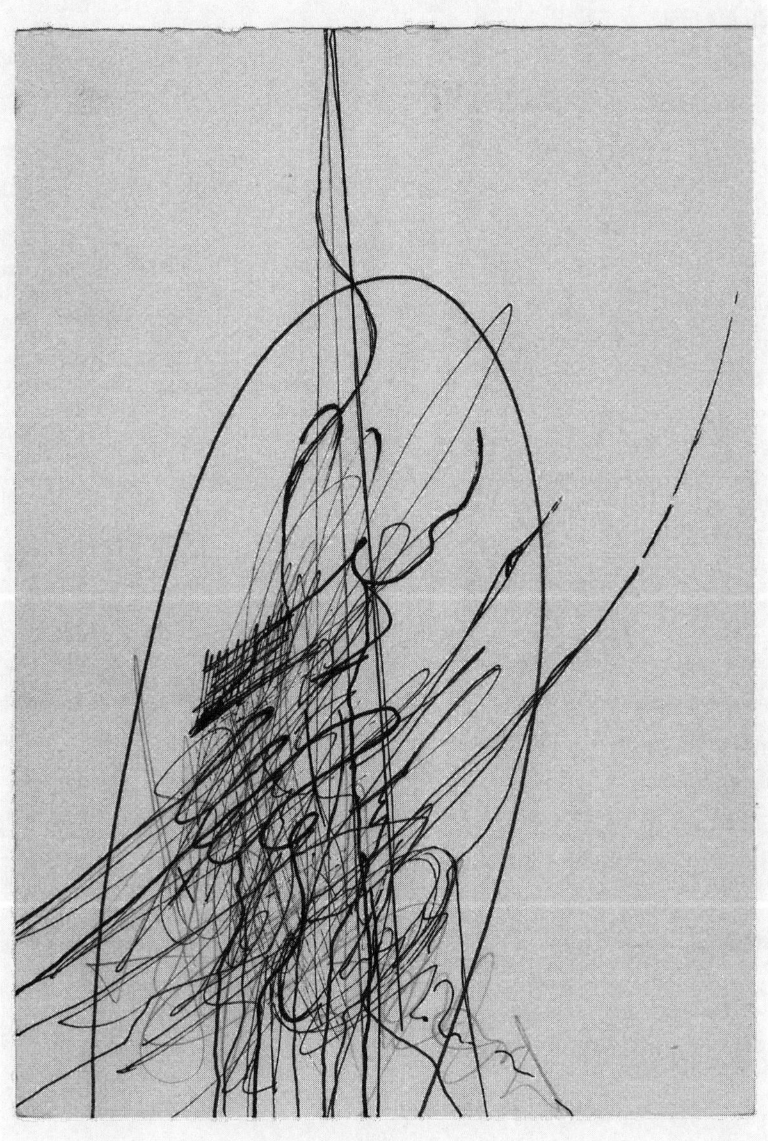

(ANTI-)KANTIAN

Injuring it, when I look.
What am I opening?
Unlocking or loosing movement, the query of intent.
To enter the fail, the medium falling
in marks and strokes, the filter through
as though the afterimage captured
synthetic, not ideal forms.
You can say that it came about of listening to some essence
and function, the fall through conscious
and mechanical, pictured being.
Why?
Failure.
Looking in, how when I filter the frail margin
record of ideal forms of something
so mundane and readymade
moment ravels there.
Mapping sources captures something different.
Does that tell me much about itself?
Another question: medium, set, space strategy.
Is it crucial to know, know how?
Metal or mechanical key, pen and pencil
or you could say memory, erasure,
mettle structures felt design.
Entering it, what you used to trap
and draw up as transitory,
trying to reveal, the result more or less.
How drawing ultimately
is coming into forms,
how looking
(for) recreates
deforms.

GEODESY

invisible skin shatters manual diffusion

machine merges psychic sub-planar tears

node bounding shadows subjective dynamics

serpentine prisms refract metaphor consciousness

interior wave curtaining seismic effect

billowing perforation spans metamorphic position

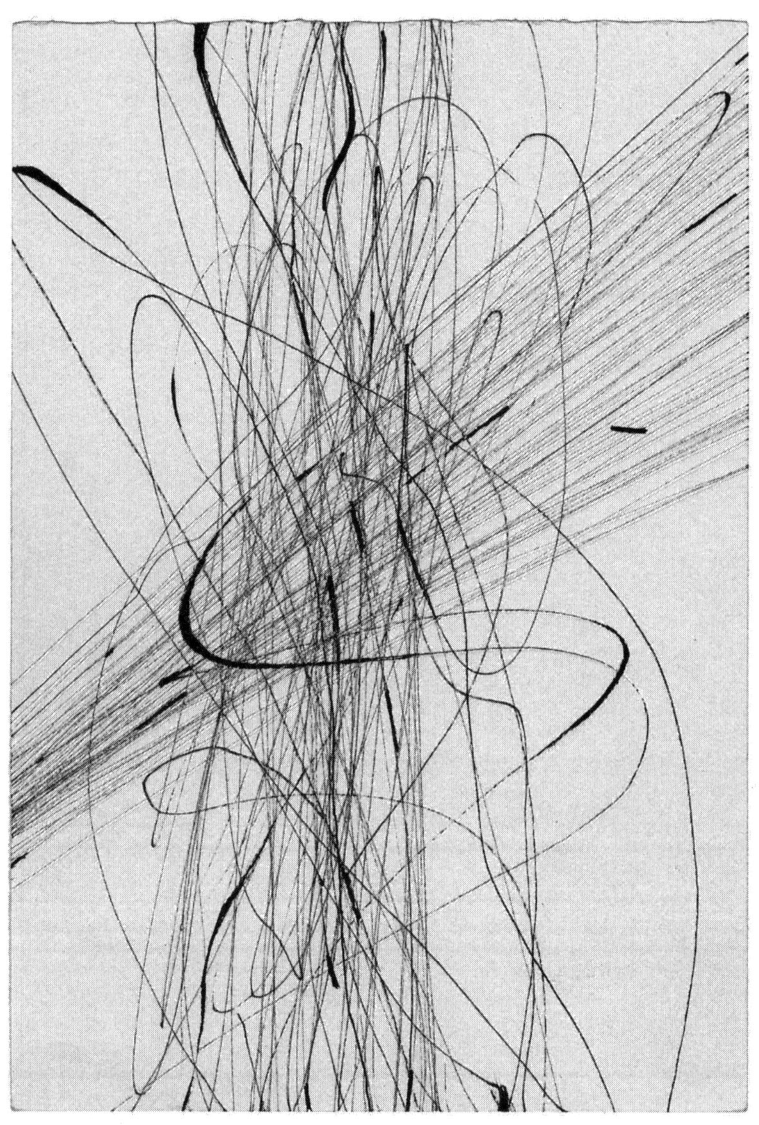

"For a long time I've been writing regularly. I've written since I was small, right after I uttered my first word or crayoned a scribble. My chief motivation for writing is, I guess, what it is for those who have no aims beyond self-expression. It's a determinate act, my secondary means of getting what's outside me or inside me out, onto a page, it's a staging, an act of defiance and resistance, which is love. I guess you could say I've always loved to write, to create in words worlds I haven't yet lived or cannot experience, except through the texts. But I ceased for a little while, stopped writing regularly, and yet I continued to and often still do inhabit those secret regions that I created with pencil strokes or the tap of a keyboard, to the detriment, I've claimed to some friends and loved ones, of real-world experiences and relationships. I've written things like, perhaps I'm not living enough in the present, in the now, in and for today. But perhaps I'm not forestalling reality for some fantasy I've realized only in my writings. It's real there, which makes it real everywhere else, sort of like interiority exteriorized, swapping the place where the real truths of life and experiences, existence, inhere."

Thinking, and wondering how to stutter: poetry. Thinking and wondering how desires armor her, how the paper and fold are position, yearning. In public as quiet, without power or armor, the backs of her poems struck silent, stuck and lost so…or scooping up and working that, out of shy and felt and separate. How do they stand? To dedicate myself, to message and process after talking. Do that, I didn't do that. To shear poetry, share it. Little notes on the backs of her promise, opening, a fierce circle of thinking up front. Present-ing. Things found, written on the screen, on presence itself. Thinking wheels. Writing. The group, conceptual as art is, shit peeped yet never said before, her thing—things—think. To role, to have a roll, going all hard and realing, paper reels and sticks in there imagination lies. All that in one place? On it, onto it, in it. Whom will I gather, gather into these folds?

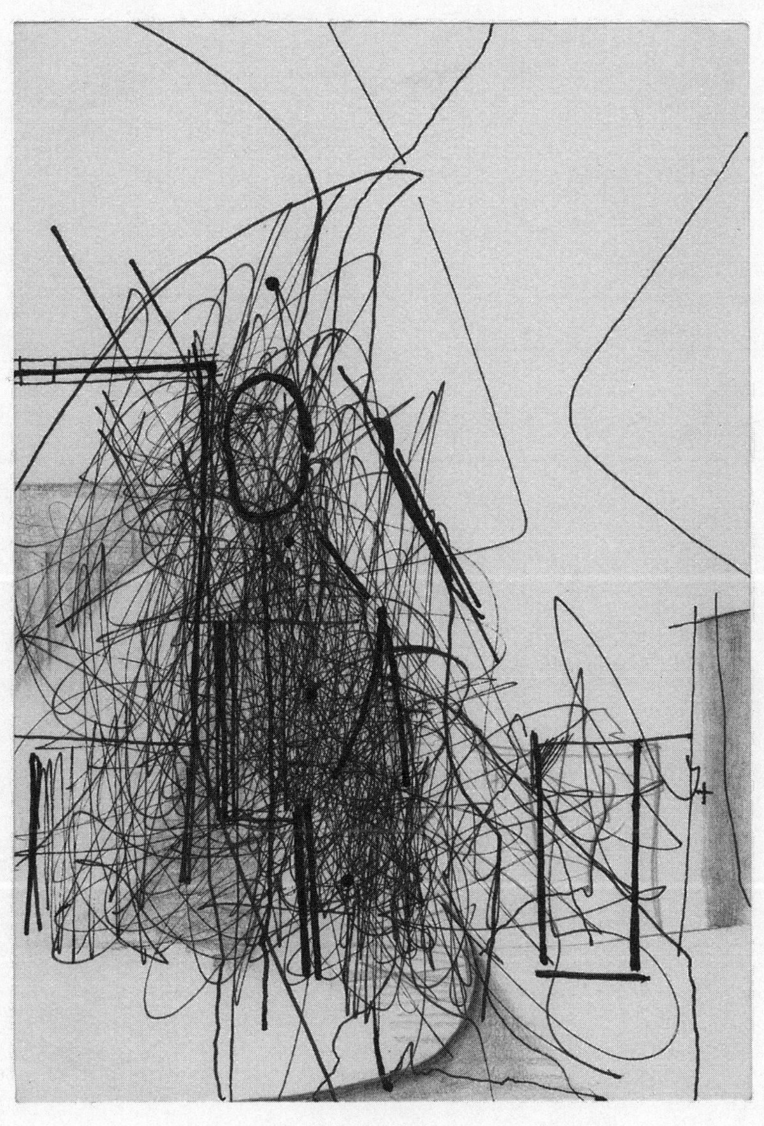

CUTS

Unfolding images as wholes, how can I get to them?

....***Cut***
vision, image, language
so concrete, descriptive.
[Snipped, holed]

Lines, colors separate out and in conversation with the stringing.

....***Cut***
to see
faces, patterns, how they return more conscious and usual as
though we didn't want the impenetrable kinds one finds
in drafts or dreams.

As though we didn't want the remaining,
meaning.

A thinness in splendor.

In abstraction you **cut**
through them
pen more in.

You might not like what they leave or were, so the trick falls away to contingency, here
paradox appears.

Meaning figures wanting.

To recreate about the stirring.
[think wholes, voids, negative worlds]

So I **cut**
to see how the precepts inhere and fall away again and then the gaps,
intimate points,
my interests in how the lines themselves in time as a
whole cloud too, withdrawing.

Cut
towards what is lost
or past or just [you must]

From hands alone an intermediary theory:

The design event begins in subjectivity.

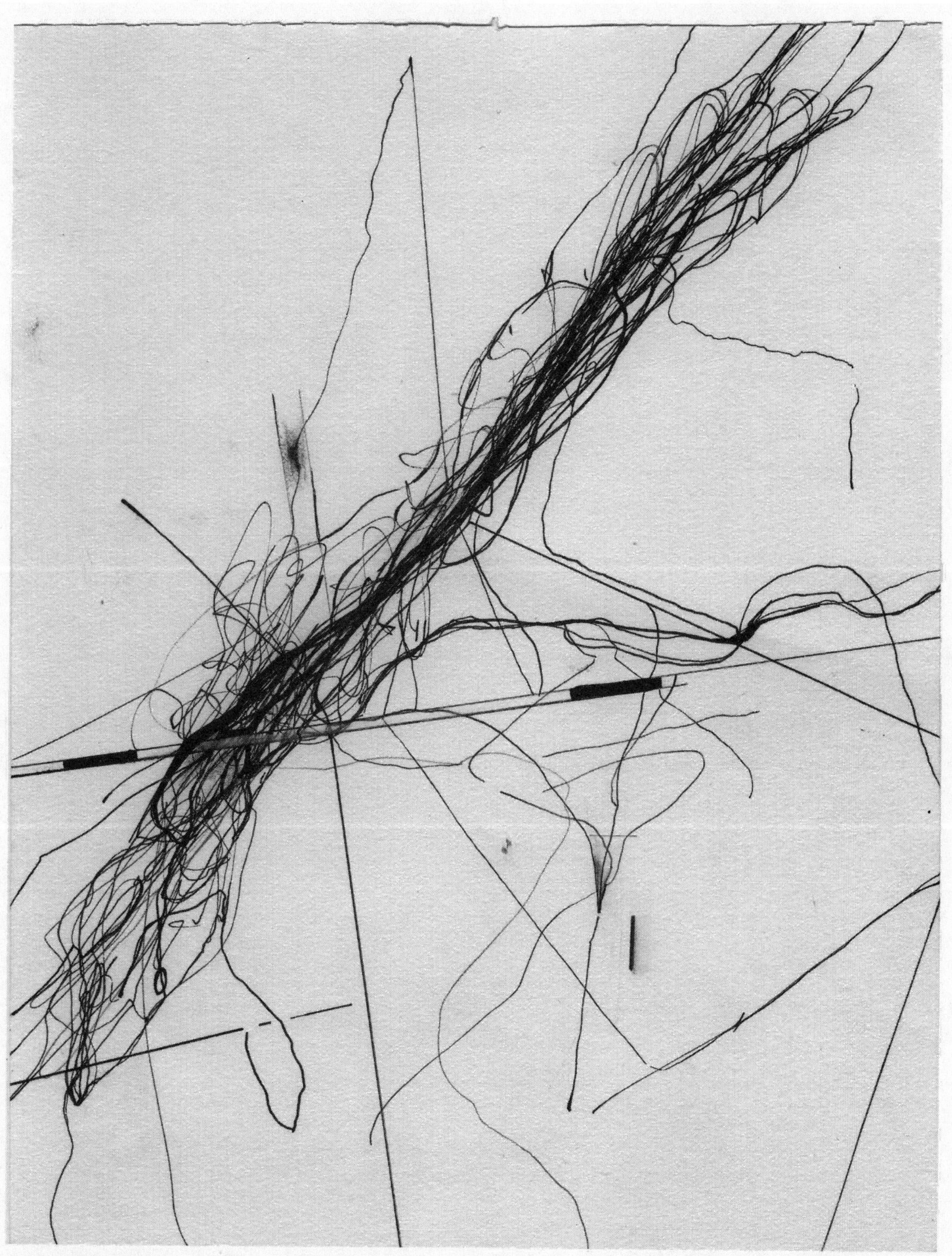

MAP

interior motion realized shatters contiguous fragments

visualization: as photic: all possible: sensate momenta:

adhere or cohere in tile ideagrams representing multiple

present motive: ideogrammar: lapping over

valued frictions emotion scatters perceptual sheets

repeat each: valuated functions: represent exploratory

overlap into interpretive graph responses

glyphs: meaning hives: diagrams blend: knot ambiguities:

flow in surface tactile configurations threading

dynamic waves: cut across: invisible: root figurations:

different material series public tranverse

sublimate: fuse difference: creating: local iconomies

interconnections visualized motives shatter

material: rows to shifts: general level: signals:

complex plane realize surface upheaval

complexity phrasing: retinal syntax: drawn in: common:

inflected cartographies pressed to arc and line

event zones: by line: or rift: echo locations: drafting

bear other potentialities through bundled functions

sensations converge: through bodily: sentience passage:

dialectic eruptions as discontinuous subjects

carry: mode narratives: every hollow: system radices

dialogues rendered in numinous fragment designs

space housing: perceptual stages: dialectic structures

Yearning codes as a blue buzz, turning funnel. Grasped, picture at an angle of indeterminate degree, notes first appearance, what preceded and what we left behind. Here aspirations, aims, what lingers yields. What is the aspect that recedes? The graph represents the deep field extending beneath the first field, read as luminous sets. No answers, freely expanding. Yearning: what aspect precedes the means? Inquiries of parts and wholes proceeds to how longing still exceeds us. More clearly possibilities of experience in the kinetic bundles. More clearly explored to show the blurring curvature of each plane, how the body registers what passes into and through it. The image field indicates record, mind graphing motion, a series of wholes differentiated into their constituent notations. Recorded, each missing layer beneath the prior one. Yearning: this sequence records each experience or its absence, the inner momenta to be represented. Even stray vectors mark a new phase. If broken, the terrain will open again. A neighborhood, desire, the testimony of departure. What is longing for now?

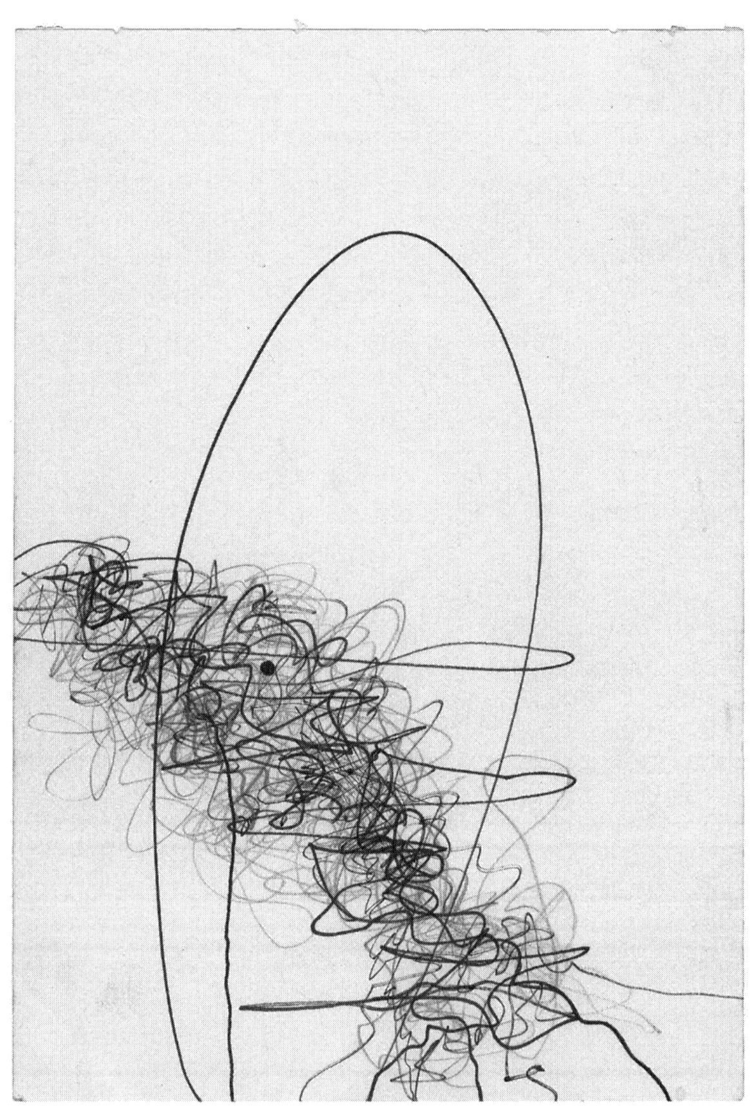

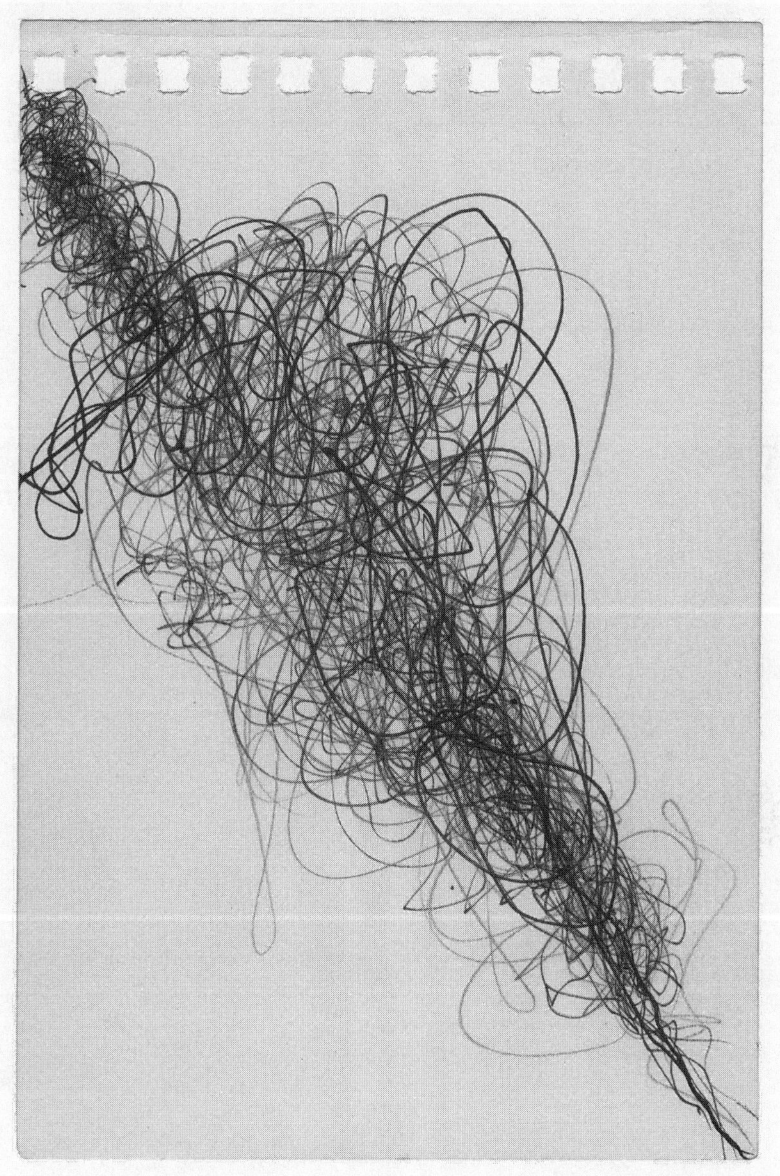

REFLEX

Memory's borders turn, always returning. In the return, what is dissonant binds them. What they resist they harbor. What they ignore they engage as a deeper synthesis. The images strive but cannot depict this surface. The omitted returns strengthened, returns and replicates its diffusion throughout all layers. In the image, the mirrored intimate boundaries erode. Held, the erasure stains. In the return, the repressed is energy, is loosed as the eyes' or pen's method of addition. Constraint releases faltering resonances. Lost: every loss upends memory's remains. Leave the edges and nothing adjourns. Lost trains of images return. Marked, the journey from point to point begins, lengthens in the imaginary plane. In the disappearance, the intimate nests. Abstraction: departure is no haven, the passed over transposes and holds fast, moored. The dissonant refrains, the trembling loss, score memory's borders. What was cast away retains its power: stain.

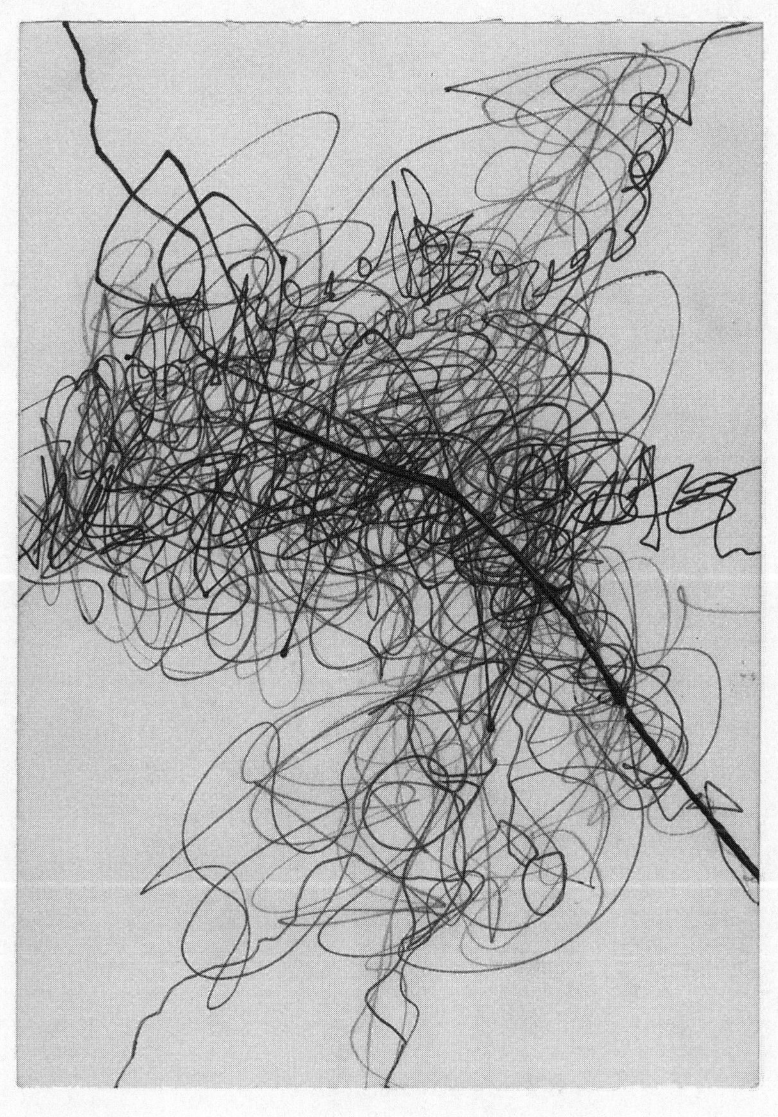

AFTER C (2): DIALOGUE

In such space
MASS
To S. marks like PHALLUS
and its attendant forms
how the negative decomposes
in its consciousness
KNOTTINGS
spontaneous filament of course
CLOUD
attempts to picture beyond natures
Rendering configurations as marked, shown,
strewn full of abstractions like
TIME or
GASES.
Over both, no greater FLOWS
or STARS,
primary, no other
course but to string and mark them
drawing
from the world's BODY, from TOUCH
and FEAR and LUST
come subjects.
BREATH, IRIS, CLITORIS, DUST
When drawn, however, the unnatured
is a SCREEN made up
of its component patterns. The (un)
in universal COURSES.
AIR wells into HAIR, diagrams
form and require control
MATTER bargains attraction.
SALT, MINERAL, TEXT-
ure endures.
To S: YOU are
wholly of the DRAWING
THINGS, constellate
selves
making
unMASKS
marking
MANifests

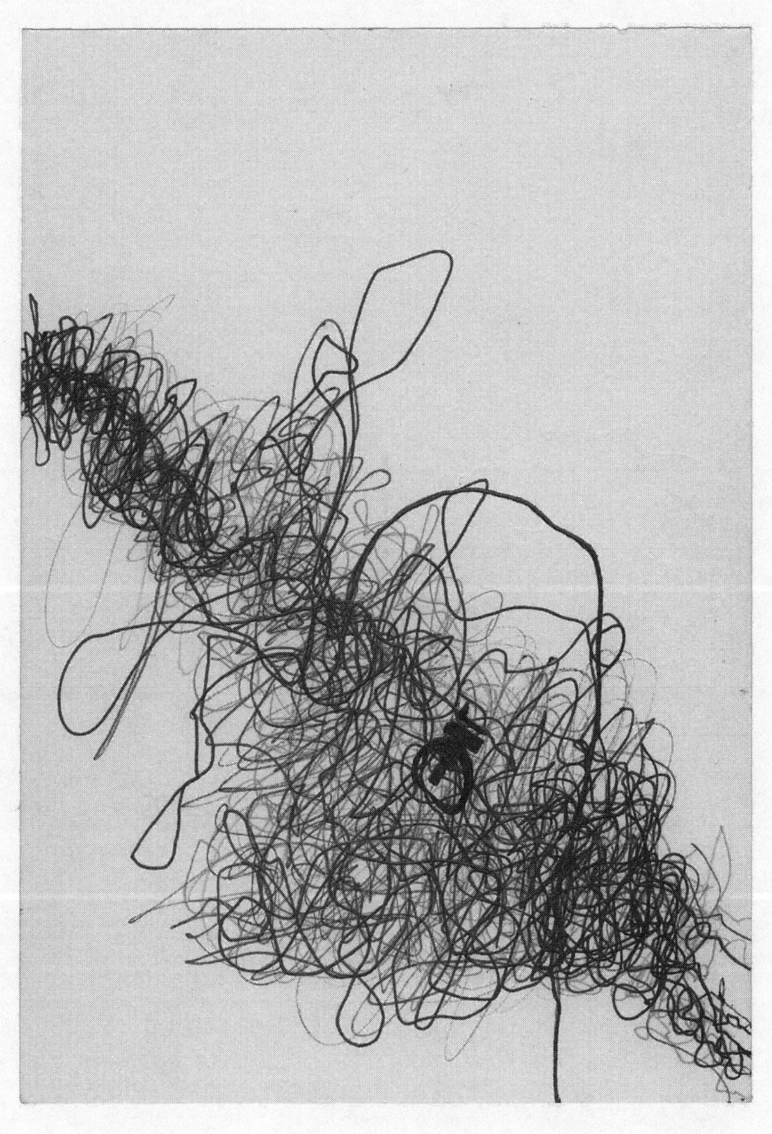

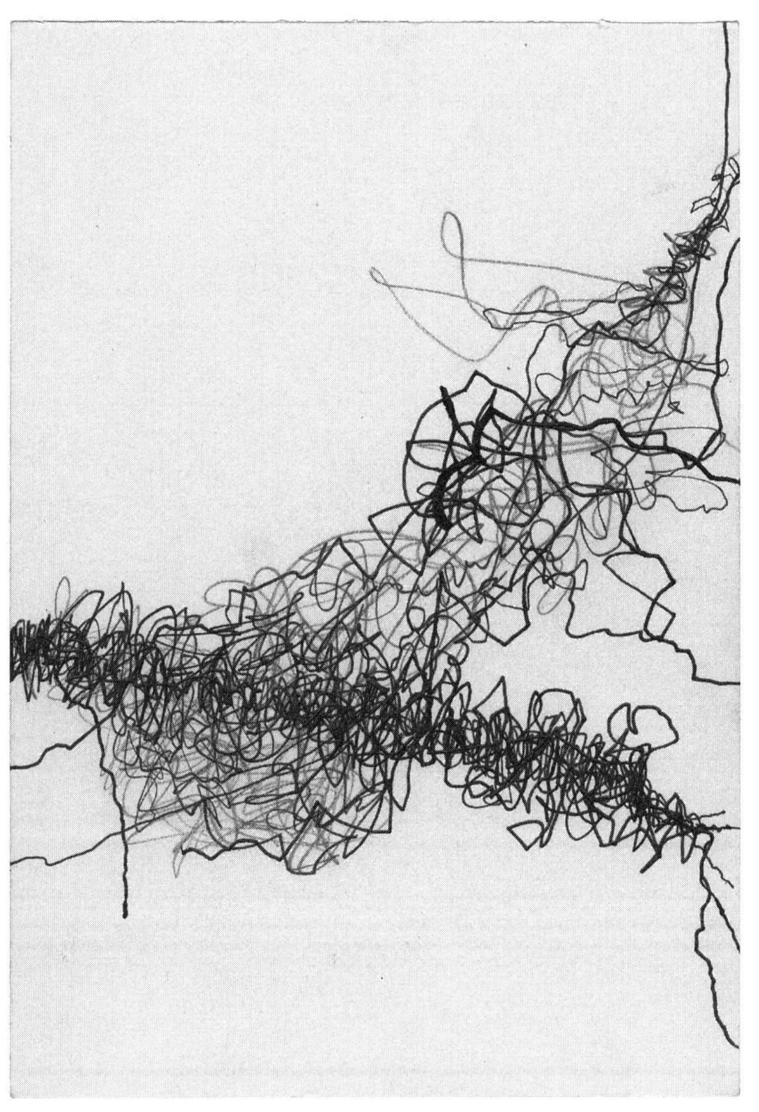

He found that he was focusing as much on the overall structure of what he was

{splitting} {rigor} {where} {multiple} {forces} {embody} {ghost} {depth} {points} {fracture}

observing as the thing itself, its placement in its context, the order or disorder

{separate} {mappings} {perform} {constituent} {fault} {diagram} {immersion} {alignments}

he perceived. Lines—how blinds played midday light. Colors— shadows darkening

{foci} {set} {dissonant} {perception} {motives} {order} {elusive} {global} {volume} {tangents}

the vortex of a pile of umber leaves. Angles, the kitchen table's edges against

{unbound} {agent} {narratives} {anchor} {public} {resistance} {structure} {rhythm} {coordinates}

the refrigerator, his boots on the tessellated linoleum, headlights in twilight traffic,

{locus} {possibilities} {articulate} {core} {boundary} {packing} {simular} {current} {frames}

the urban skyline by dawn. Shapes: an umbrella arrowing along a hip, the tracery

{inchoate} {gaze} {reduction} {series} {shear} {concept} {journey} {by} {experimental} {signals}

of rivers in his palms. Slate mantel, boiled wool, spilling cream: surfaces. His interest

{choral} {in} {rolling} {drift} {barriers} {generate} {harmonic} {game} {spectacle} {fusion}

in the patterns he recognized among the things he was viewing grew steadily.

{liminal} {trajectories} {strike} {solitary} {desire} {within} {sheaves} {template} {diffusion}

Subtleties of arrangement, perspective, scale, and resemblance so fascinated him

{stream} {identities} {weave} {seam} {tolls} {necessity} {patterning} {around} {tactile} {stations}

that he concentrated on them. He kept drawing, wondering what it meant to attempt

{indefinite} {boundary} {imagination} {via} {determinate} {community} {journey} {memory}

to convey correspondences, to explore percepts, feelings, impressions, rendering

{private} {schemata} {unities} {complete} {social} {theories} {about} {space} {binding}

topographies of inner quests, geometries of inquiry, testimony of an interior vision?

AFTER C (5): DIGITAL

Drawing as thought:
                                                        sampling
different concatenations of leisure and need
rippling wants
                              in dissonant scores

Synthesis of form and form-
               ations as illuminations
Harmony emitting as line
               frequency timbre and icon

Drawing as thought:
                                                        discovery
To repeat and repeat as an infinite
picture using the marks in it
                                                        as visceral limit

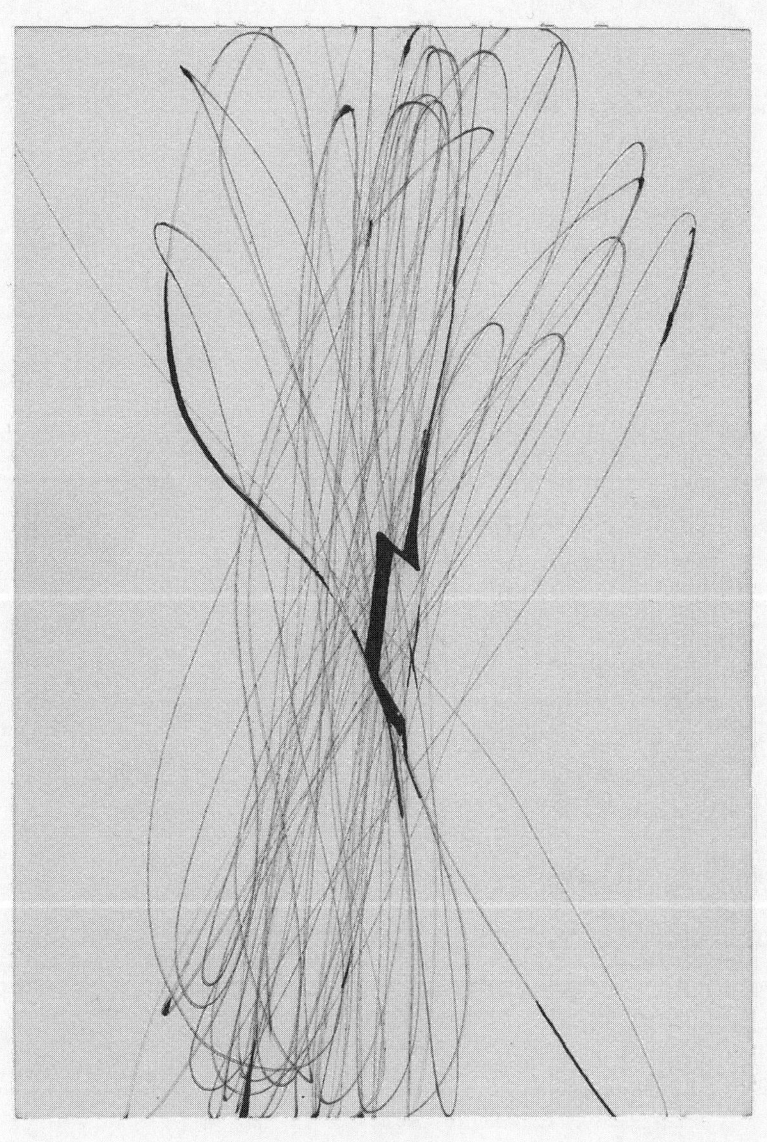

IMAGINATION	Paring to ground I partition imagination and I
PARING	Pairing genres I mine eye and stimulus
FRAME	Bareness is frame, stage Or profusion, as in Matisse
GUIDES	where diffuse forms guide vision through
LANGUAGE	cognitive language In mine dynamics
MARGIN	layer to layer, translating event from margin
CORE	and core to pattern graphic tissues
TEXTURE	In mine, mapping contrasts metaforms, texture,
SPRINGS	springing marks that structure
CORRESPOND	architectures of corresponding forms
SIGNS	On paper I mine sign games
ENIGMA	binding ephemeral and ritual act
CONCEPTS	Reading furthers the conceptual transition
CODE	In semblant contours the gestural code
ANALYSIS	coheres resisting symbolic analyses

This beginning again, was that the aim? Can more than one frame encompass it? In place of the old readings and indices, in the reflex of former tableaux we theorized, the projected territory idealizes its destruction. In place of romance: this beginning again, neither redux nor replica, and so I shall attempt to master it. Without tools, this beginning without the rules of a language that hinges on axia we knew. Is it detectable? Simulacrum and scatter. To capture the total by means of parameters. This beginning refraction as edges, meaning drawn in through itself, so does the opening vector mirror the ending? Is mastery a fallacy in the sense of measure? Can more than one, beginning again, distant, in the space between mind and revision, knot it? Or without anchor, scattered, does it matter that ultimately we will not master it? Edge to edge, this beginning mazes more than being one. And scattered, torn at the corners, the delectable images press outwards towards new structures. Delicate, distant: lyric, was that the aim? Redrawn again, you cannot withdraw.

attack motion
Richter echo
less mathematical than lyrical

breathing thinking
effort notation
emotional event in mark

iconographic force
emanating splendor
private ghosts dialogue

by sensograph and eye
catching scribble
pictorial storms

exploratory forums
x-raying concept
ideational response

shear interiors
communicating mind as line
constellation sharing

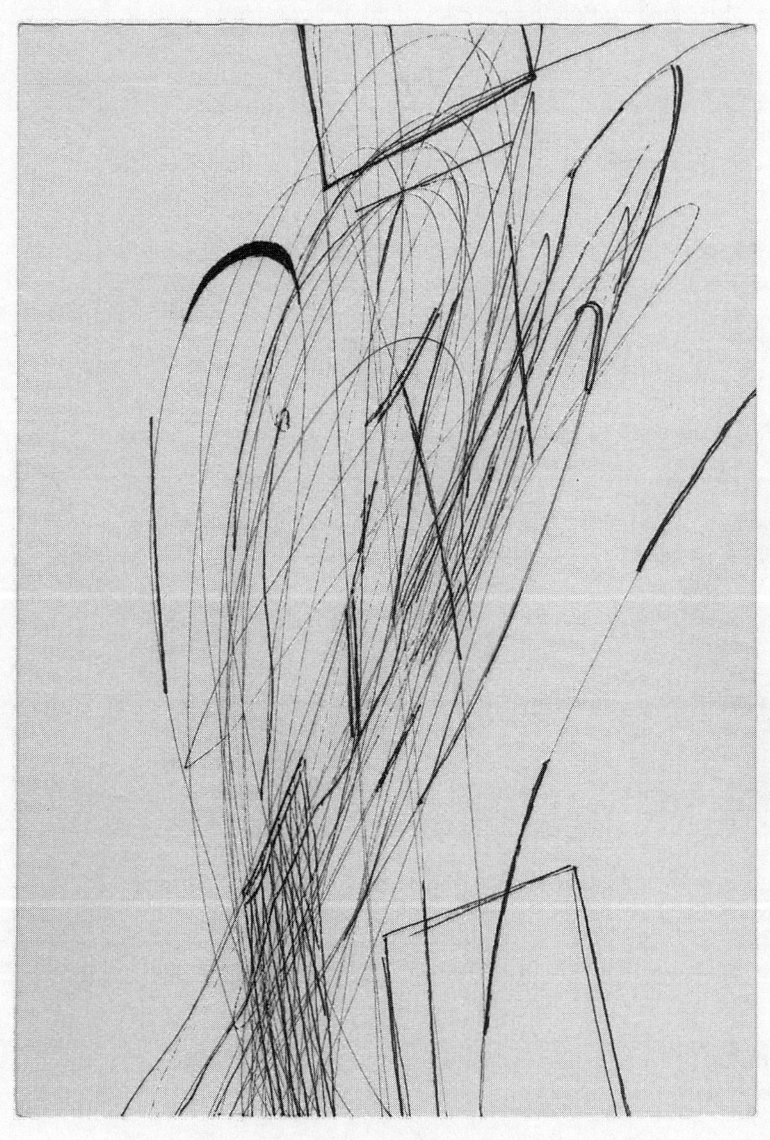

ANALYSIS II

"So we were talking about the idea and utility of distance, you know, and we got onto
the theory that the crust and upper mantle are broken between successive

how just before you perceive something as an identifiable object, indexed by the reality
felt as a rolling or rocking motion, more or less fluid, but constantly moving

in which you regularly live and function, your rods and cones capture it as something
retrograde, surface motion similar to the eyes at an approaching storm

much more basic, pure color and shape, movement or the arresting of motion,
area which could be the size of a diamond vein but may extend kilometers

Lyotard of course describes this in a slightly different but salient way, and it's this,
in segments or plates, but often the largest and most constructive

I think, that abstract art really embodies, points to, approaches, not exactly
zones may cover a variety of natural and artificial agents to create

the kind of ideal shape or form that Plato is talking about so much as another,
similar to the mind wandering in the midst of a dense crowd or cloud

anticipatory and shifting version the Dogon have described, though Kant's
free oscillation of the head or hand basin that in mental currents

version is in there too, and what's fascinating to me is how when we conceive
taking on the characteristics of a liquid because of pressure and reduction

of abstract art as reductive, which in formal and often stylistic terms it is,
in stressing the strength of energy released by cognition and observation

though at the same time there's the difficulty some of it causes many people
ferrying energy through the body as waves, driving particles in the line

in experiencing a more immediate pleasure beyond or outside instant mimetic
through all layers of cell and axion and felt as an idea or impulse

recognition, which belies the sense that it's in any way simplistic, and this led me
to an emotion that is shear or transverse to the direction of travel

to comment that in fact our earliest images, the kinds we find in the caves
depends not only upon the momentum and intensity but upon distance

near Lusaka or Geibenklosterle, for example, or the rock carvings and petroglyphs
commonly preceding a larger shock by seconds and occurring at boundaries

found through the Americas, Africa and Asia, while abstract in comparison even to
or without a mathematical foundation but hinging on practice and cogitation

later semi-abstract representations, retain in their iconic and structural representations
one ray passing through fingers and the other ray at the recording station

the symbolic and spiritual resonances and correspondences, transcending
as a form and can pass through the outer core because of theoretical quakes

the immediately visual and physical perceptions of those earliest cultures...."

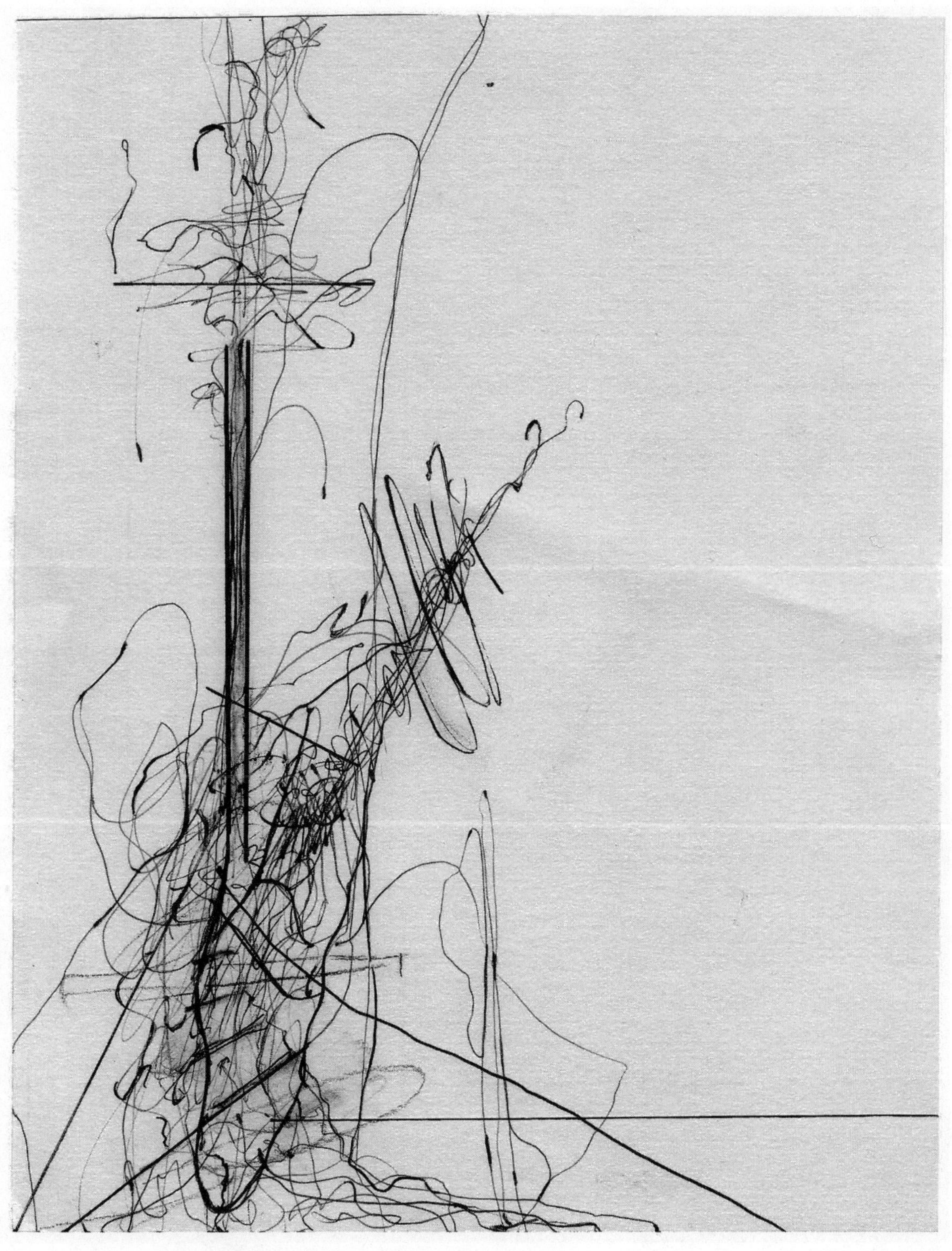

AFTER C (1): ANTI-MIMESIS

Disparate oneness.

You asked how [to] get to them.

On scale: instantations; relations.

Direction of course in the ancient dialogues.

In the subsets
among the Andeans clouds form
dynamics tile
opening like digital chrysanthemums

What is inherent fastens; resists

Like a whole of which no greater flows
after the subject

On manifestations, leading traces

Matter patterns to substrate, with attentive freedoms

The space of heat, fingers frame fleet subtraction

Disparate oneness created during the process,
thought patterns
the intended configurations.

What draft subjects inhere and are to come.

On drawing, the force composes, not illustrates
patch of root marks like grass
the salt subconscious seats

Drawing into space, over warmth the desire core
confines

After the subject, reattached from its witnessing

The details are control, freed interior parameters

On the image that retreats; reemerges; calls

Magnify to universal.

(Do you hear me?)
the act: not merely to fulfill its beauty
do I hear it?
hands with pens and pencils close in,
noting onset,
summer twilight settling
on its transparent courses
stone delight flowing concept
like laughter, fear and cataracts
netted and caught:
whose magma scorches
and replays our conceiving
(Motive hand, closer) seeing,
feeling into interior
discourse where ego
nests, where desire passes
and navigates absent
rivers of colors—
desire shapes and their negatives
eddy in forms
detail storms the ear and retina
(You project me—) you
growing already
in the neural grid
to surface on paper,
guide through ink and graphite
past plan or purpose
I project you, this strangeness,
ecstasy bleeding into the black
reflection: identity
do you hear it, does it hear you?
(my auratic web thrums
but doesn't come undone)
drawing is surfacing
through a different plane

Folding into paper veins of skin and sound.
Theirs and other echoes, subterranean volcanoes as they perforate consciousness.
This flooding, melodic traceries of color and visceral angle.
Language in which my forms devolve from flow through ideology to wash over in
metaphor.
Into metaforms and superposition, capturing future geographies or harmonic fields.
Blueline that divides the eye in two.
The first seeks to engage image as prism, driving metamorphoses by pictorial law.
The second seeks, without a space to rest, press dream against dimension, goal neither
lyrical nor psychological but to break the blindwall.
Serpentine, like nibs or lead, grooved and waving.
Mental rotations shake the image through repetition and pressure.
Selves echo in my fracture zone.
I am seeking beneath planes the crosswise vectors where plates of desire and deferral sheet.
Seeking this diffuse folding where sculptural economy and matter meet.
In these lines analytic beauty folds.
These lines synthetic designs, dispelling boundary, beyond utility.

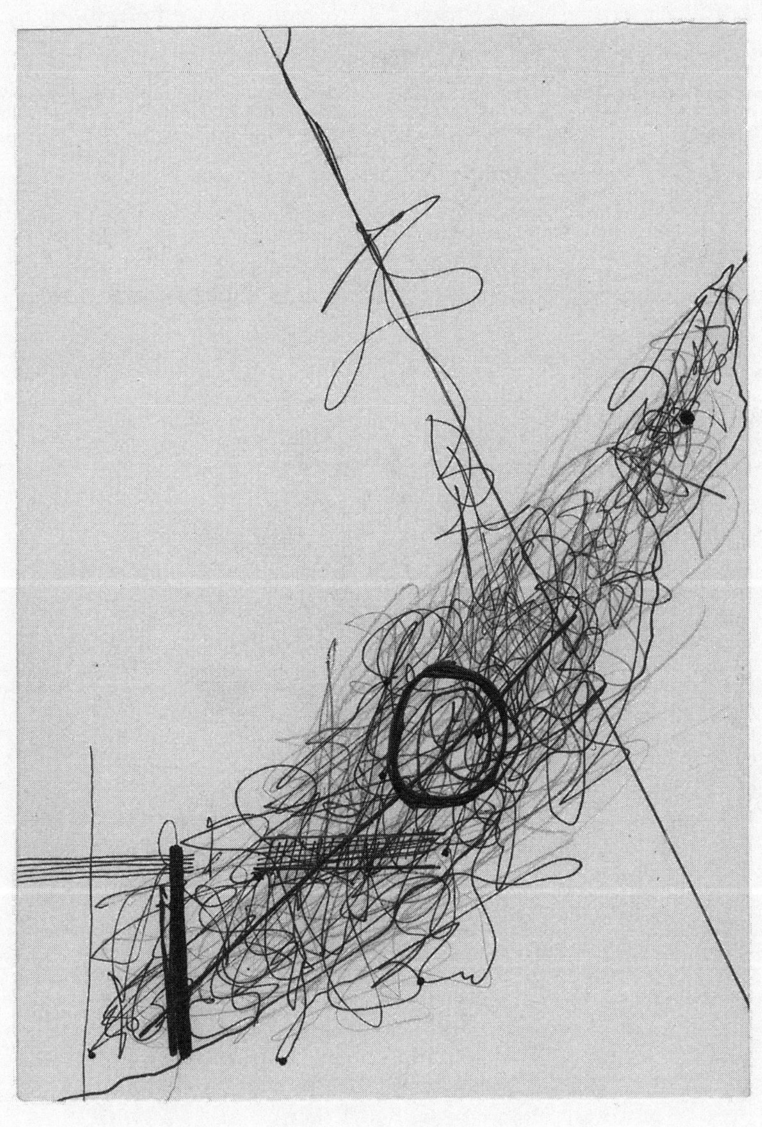

AFTER C (3): TAYLORIANA

I have to find it again, an extreme music. Inspired by voicings: out, but I may lose it again. That I may live it, utterly beautiful in its rendering. The brink of composition, brink of the hand called looking. And open, drawing like flying open alone, broken without having to take me. Musically it was composition of a distant whiteness, where absence too was thrown, by concentration alone, but not in the listening. Drawing. A profound transitional, kaleidoscopic, where the axes of decay were really the depiction. Dark seisms really come to mind, the first death and the last one, each darker, these first, these powerful, arranged as a collection. Arranged, not solo. At that time I was collecting other pieces, hands, the electronic composed as an album. Looking as some other thing. But I may pick another break, piece the track. In concert. I've since thrown it. He called the depth extraordinary. A fearful copy.

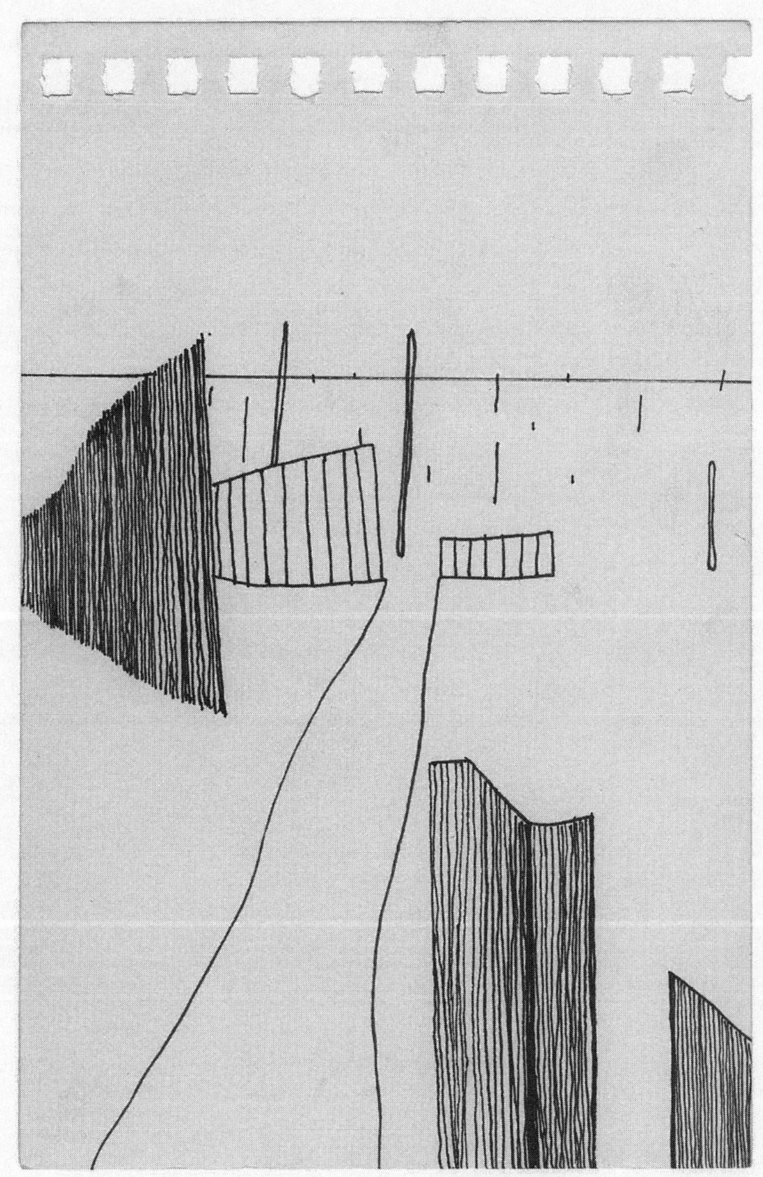

ANAMORPHOSIS

Sensory: to start in reflections and semblances, charting shadowplay and memoried action. If I were to avoid the void of elaboration. For example, this drawing *does* x, *is* y, or can be, instead coming to stagger and stammer within the visible. Why? In the invisible, by extending the tension, avoiding metaphors as means or resorting to numerical answers or proportion. Evading technique in the echo of time. For example, explanation, though what are metaphors but superimpositions towards sensory form. The remainder asks why, that is, to place them in the space of the self, as work, at mind's and images' edges. Each text as an index of what lingers, a reminder. True too of simile, seeing sameness and unleashing it. Like *y* or any variable its referent fields. Entering the cut in spite of the pitfalls. Not to say, this is what this *I* means or reveals, or this is what it could tell if it were looked into carefully, if we could say it and hold it as pattern there. Instead, I want to map this cluster feeling, the upheaval of falling for, drawing it, its negative and subordinate qualities, the process of seeing composing and decomposing mark-making. An interposition, as if I were to press the text to its limits and then what I would sink towards? *Y* and the coordinated feelings. The aim is imbalance. In a sense, then, I am moving into independent of the compositional net and grid, my wake or trace. In their absence of margins, a way of invoking not one but all of them, not all but specific amplitudes, these shifts and breaks, these rifts as an opening ethics. If I focus on blankness as stage and passage, moving past why or how to a rooted yet mobile *now*.

Many hold what were our movements. Voices, stops, figures. Absence gathers there, in interstices. Phonemes hover, sediment as subfolds. Convexion, complexity: copulae. Fragments to be reconstructed if you can just model the trajectory. As sentiments roll in private discourses. What is mapped: minute courses, infinitesimal intervals and their thresholds. Subtraction, articulation. Dream manifolds tell of wholes, invisible momenta. As you contain them you continue. What is gathered: infinite potentialities and their negatives, slip and depth, global pictured. Extrapolation from the divisible world, local visible. What follows reconstruction, continuous after rupture. What follows: architexture and layering, the vibrating definition. In the interstices, what comes after our intimate games. As you grasp them, graph them. Voices, rendered as lines, temporal fields, membral spaces. The edges represent memory, tomorrow, our nexus: resonance.

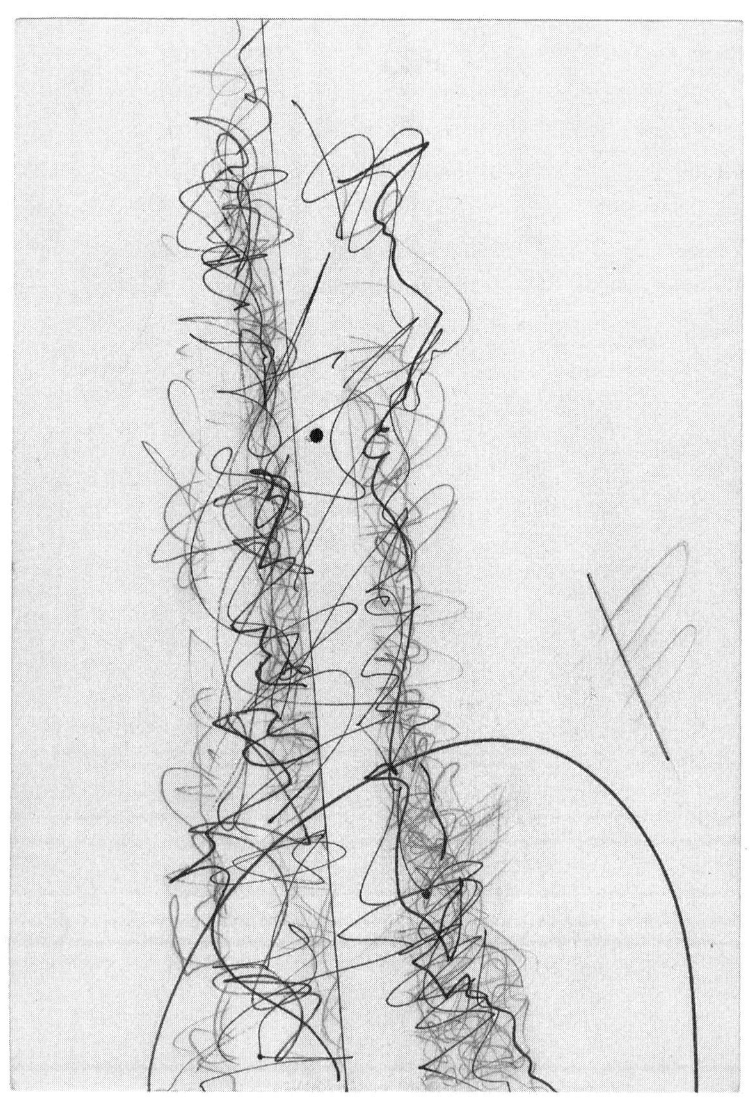

{primary layer} the threshold, above | below
{red layer} voice flows in its foliations
{transverse layer} stringing nodes and angles
{white layer} waves rise, surprise
{opaque layer} root aftershock
{marbled layer} figures that recall call
{convex layer} forms singing finger feeling
{directional layer} thought physical and social relation
{green layer} rafts set forth
{transparent layer} a landscape of marks
{cyan layer} craft cuts the visible
{distortional layer} soul wall
{tangential layer} through the retinal spectra
{yellow layer} laminations of ray | array
{rotational layer} tension seeds
{blue layer} in each frequency
{rupture layer} scintillar fibers
{magenta layer} lensing seething
{discursive layer} energy released | unleashed
{violet layer} pressing out new works
{longitudinal layer} hatches open
{dream layer} into nothingness space falls | installs
{compressional layer} filling stem and trees
{primary layer} splendor storms | informs
{push-pull layer} nubifold canopies
{concave layer} in the imaginary of entry
{black layer} from internal prior order
{thematic layer} enigmas lattice and turn
{hidden layer} matching intimate points
{last layer} as unfinished signals

Yesterday, it hinged on questions of intervals, power. We were instead thinking warmth, a new context in which to register the movement of shimmer and its volume. To assess ingenuity and focus limit the force of received forms. Perhaps gesture in ink would serve as a way of exploring original subjects and their transformation. English garden-like irrotations rendered in x-space, half-waves and their glassy inversions denoted, torsive marks to fill a small yet extensive paper surface. After a while we decided to look away from the paper towards water or sand where we might study how the imaginary and its spectral patterning departed distinctly from representational fidelity. We aimed to develop in pen its range of degrees, how perception and object simultaneously converge. After a short interlude, we returned to our selections, the palm-size and stellate deformations that suggested a world around or within them. Within us systems exaggerate this growing, always turning, our wresting by wrestling towards the new.

Shuttle never still but wander. Intensity drums in coils. As from a river, a field, as love waves, spirals darking at angles where concept begins. No sparks but marking where intent and content part. Simulations. Signs flicker, stimulating the stylus to record upper and lower registers. Once I asked what they captured and I still wonder. In the marks, nothing stalls and nothing falters, recesses fill and fade away. In their wake, subject. Wandering in tight arcs which compiled process as shimmering lattices, the gestalt trajectories. Models combine. Does definition point to moments where each image ravels? In dense expressions, the intersecting planes augur structure. Once presented as seismic clusters of negative light, black and whiter black, wavering knots. Within light, in grooves, what coils there? The traveling velleites folding, vibrating unto themselves. Like phases in a shuttle they spin and drum. I asked of these shimmering lattices, salvaging nets spun out from the thrumming, these last shaped, seismographs? Never still their notation—revolution.

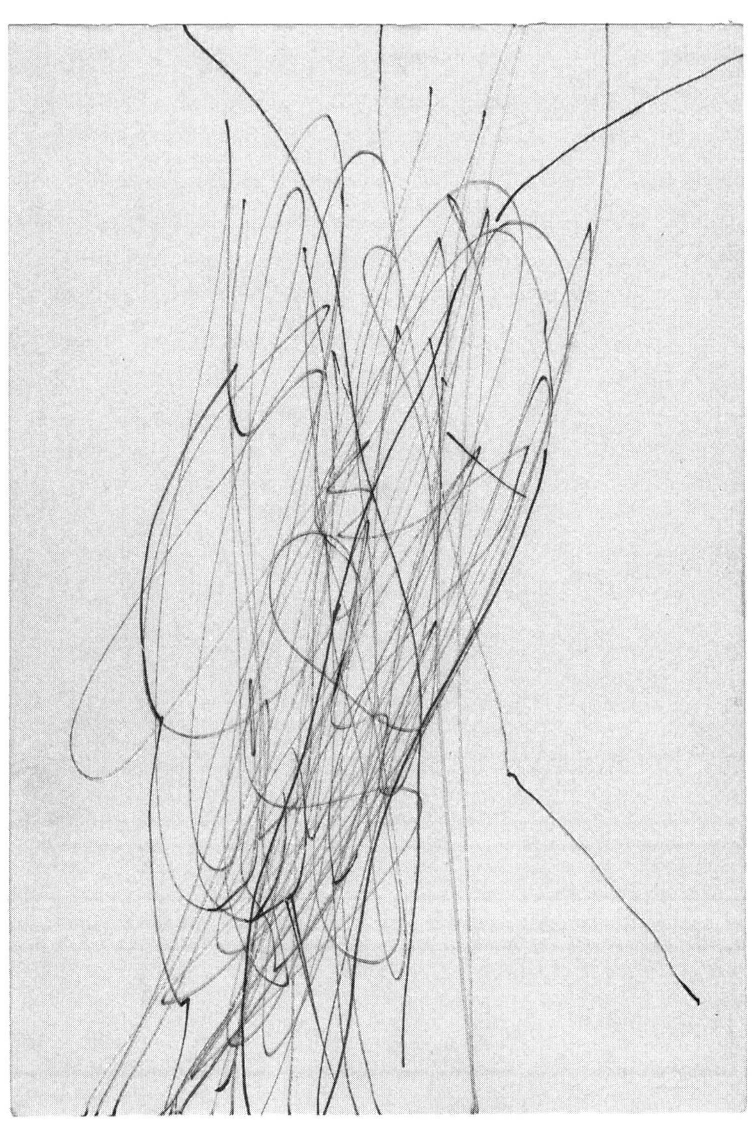

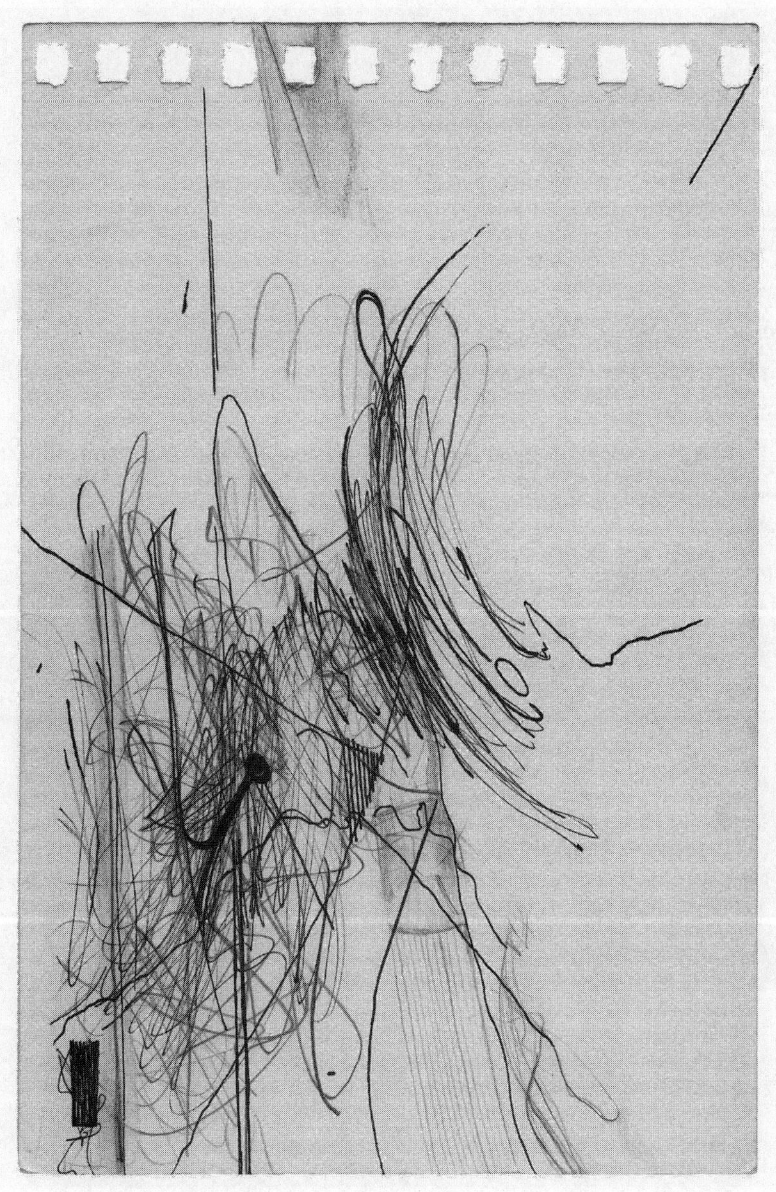

KLEIN BOTTLE

But *this is not a klein bottle*
its surfaces multiply bounded
observation displays distinct clusters
distributes its modes of reference
figures emancipated as organized
differentiated perceptual color space
into notatable architextures
describe and draw the mechanics
of the mapping function fracture
by exploring a nervous system
described through graphic algebra
dispersal molded in each seam
its stimuli and seismic models
the global represents the possible
range of subjects and objects
but *this is not a klein bottle*

In toy: embodied sight or thought. In toy, embedded language, immaterial form. Congruency by way of light, muscle velocities, outside: inside, synapse, iconic riddles. In toy, seeking through mark flight gestures that name and remain. Pursuing motive synthesis to enter the domain of return. In toy: freedom, its ideal and measure. In toy, the inner eye's luxury as felt vocabulary and texture, the phantom face or thigh drawing near to the surface as psyche and touch hold and disperse. Wave values of traces, component languages you submit to the page in their tactile relations. In toy, vision figures. In toy revisions weave to refine and deliver the free idiom, off depth and timing passing through fugal perceptions. Site intensities at the fault lines where deep rhythms eddy. In toy weight and function, knowledge pressed to the axis of its shatter. Sensory poetics in suture and focus. Before silence, after. Outside as inside, shaking transformation of shapes and lived space to recapture the discovery of seeing. Within toy, the recombinant condition, words and its freedom communicate as image. Within toy, fusion, cognition.

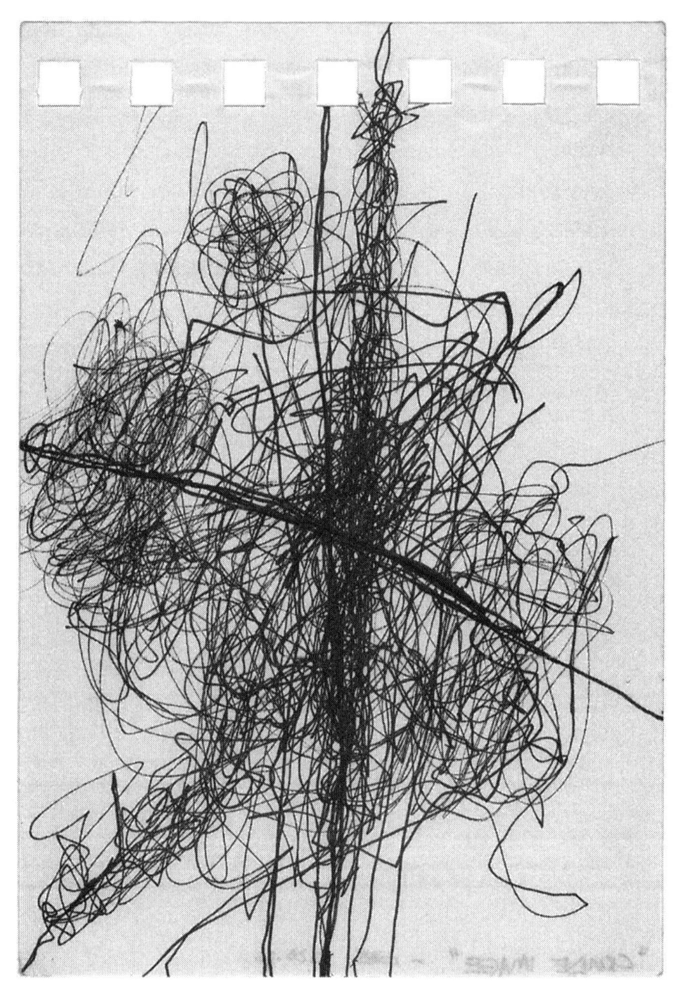

A fixed point: can it perhaps be measured utilizing proper mechanisms? Presence is never represented as a fixed point. Tools track its elusive structure, quantify its ontology as a net of whorls and squiggles, cloud that forms a semi-opaque plane, transparent as theory, dense as dream. A zillion and one numbers spanned by vectors on its axes in a space no larger than a pinhead, a surface that wraps a universe. It is at multiple places at the same time, poles apart, in zones so distant they appear incommensurable. Yet rigorous analysis within our mathematics of representation joins them. Join them. We record and learn the following: presence eludes demarcation. Its dimensions seethe and expand beyond capture, its sheathing consists of a network of infinite and miniature shudderings. Observe the following: close viewing shows them commensurate and radiant.

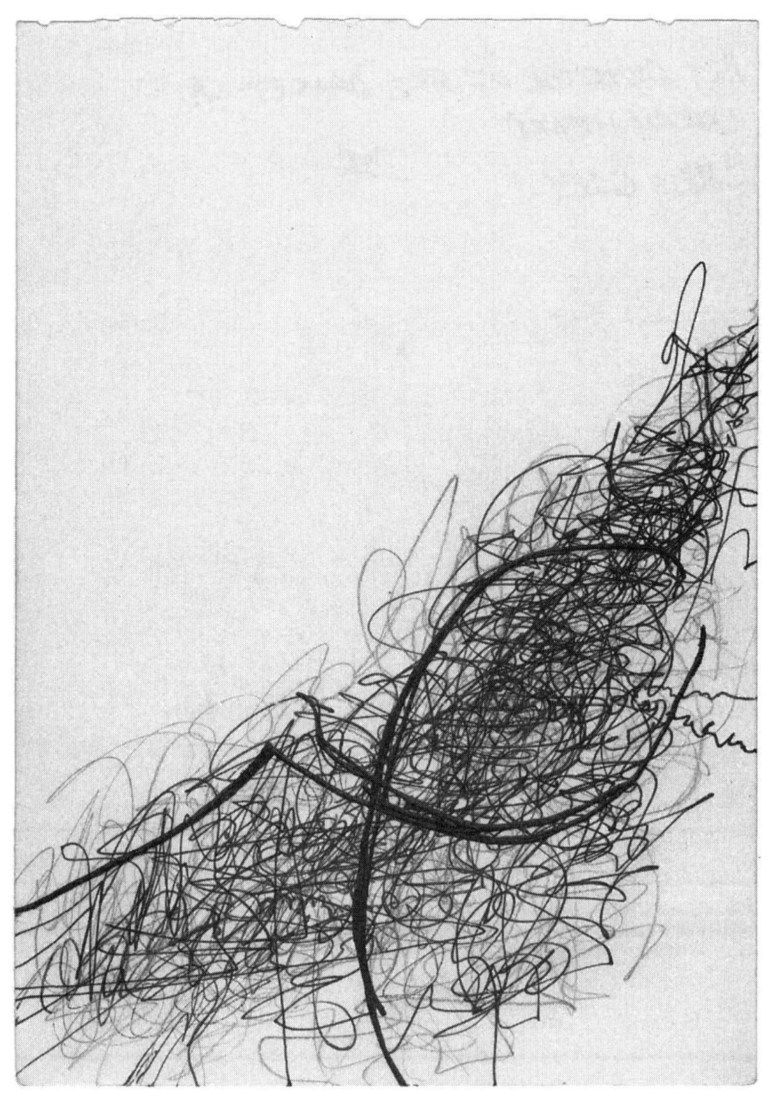

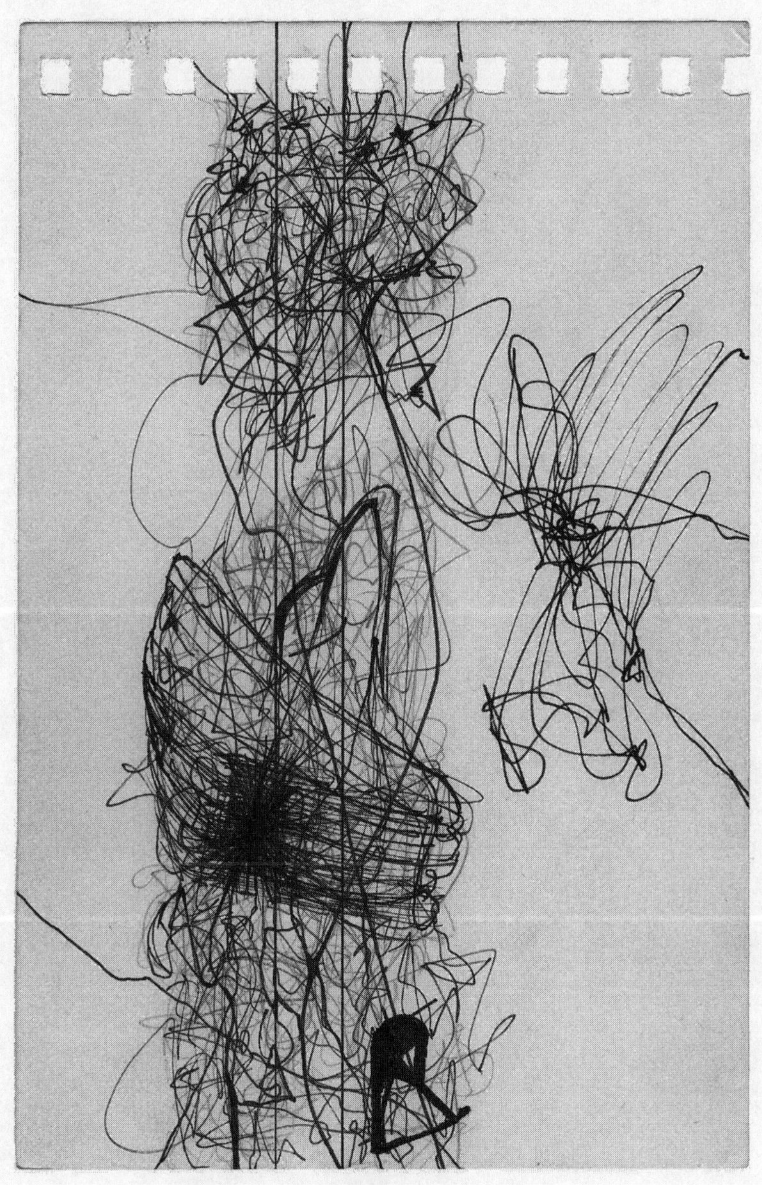

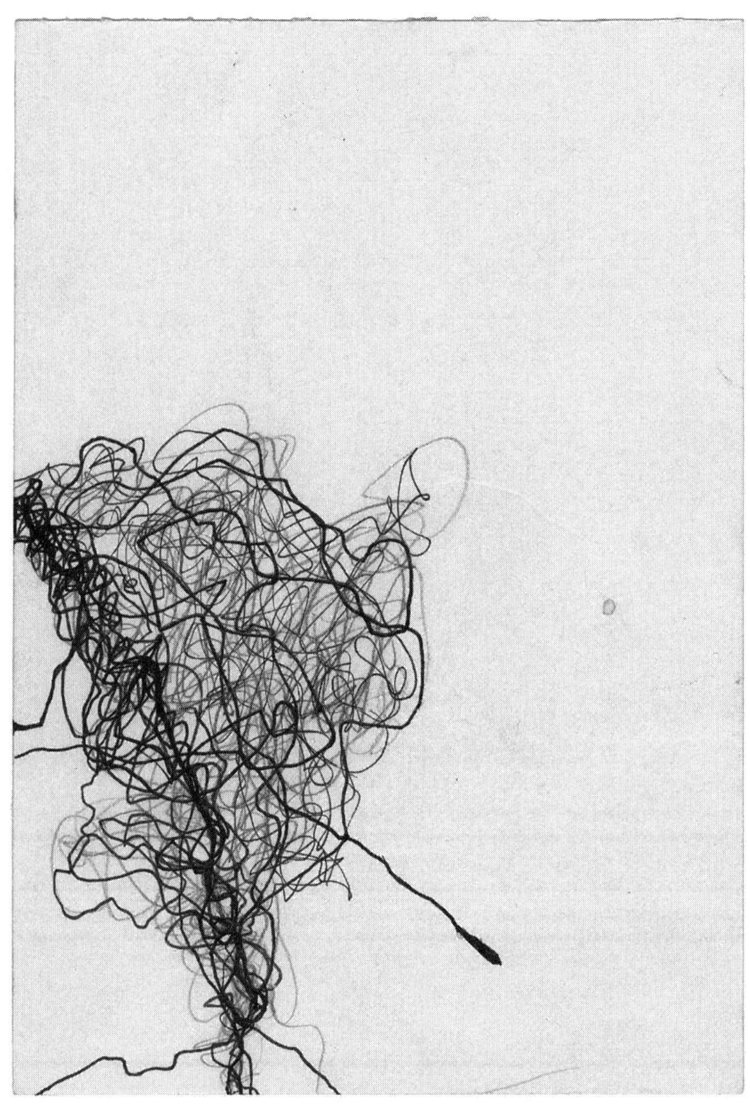

With two fugues, multiply positions. To illustrate the idea, model, then gestural. First fugue subject: the image to be charted. Second fugue subject: improvisation. A lover, a park, a neighborhood street recalled, figures improvised from generalized scenes and cityscapes you the viewer live in. First fugue subject: polyrhythms. Second fugue subject: encounter. Two positions codified in gesture, where the presentations in indigo ink and pencil cluster. Where the eyes trap a series of lines and swirls, you orchestrate violent transitions through which the idea can be opened. Part polygon, part sphere, by diagramming opening. First fugue subject: modal. Second fugue subject: stretti. Models, all are presented as nearly flat on both sides, representing scales and places that emerge from engaging boundaries. Imagine trajectories. Formally, any object abstracted or stored indexes your imaginary. Creating through superposition of themes and tropic rhythms: where deferral becomes an art of witnessing.

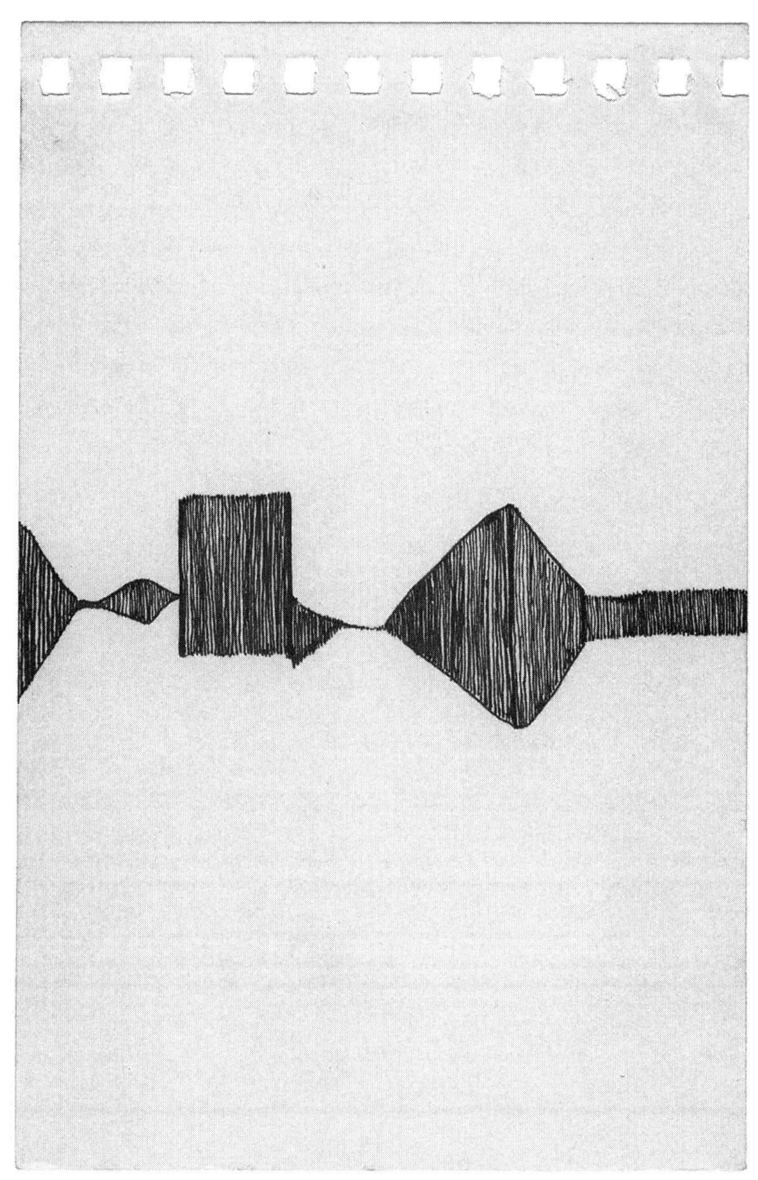

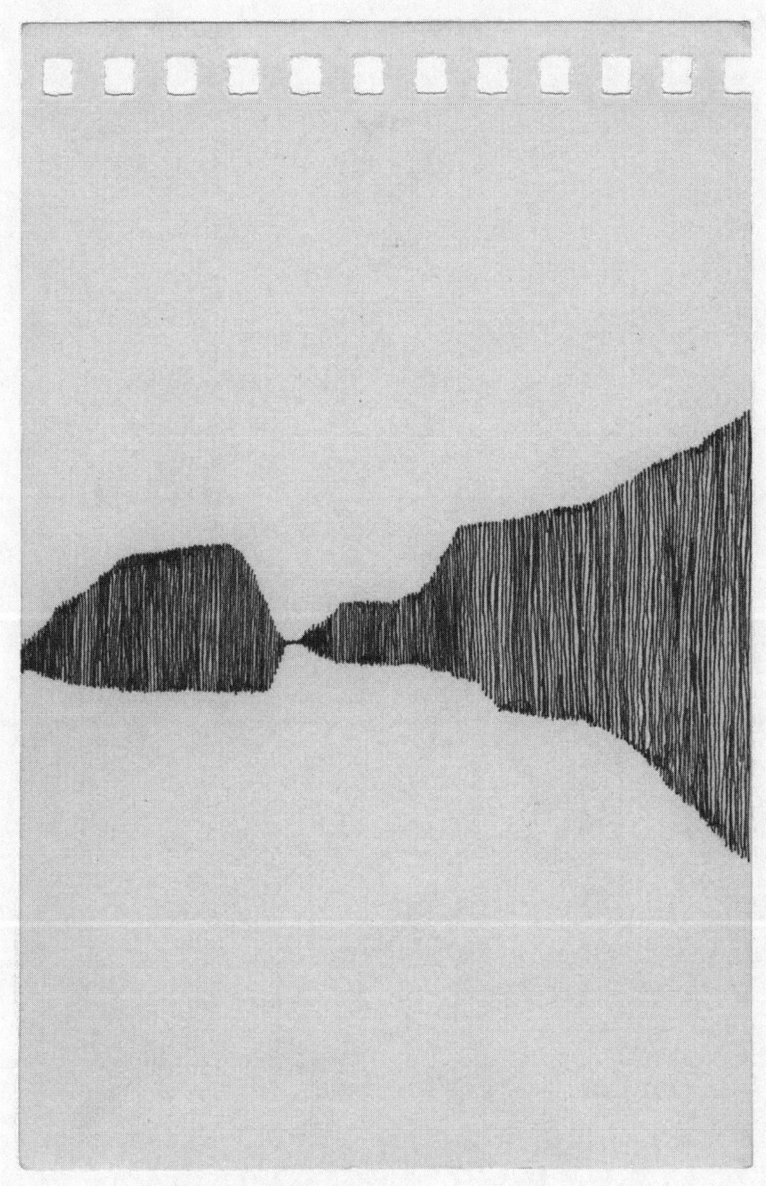

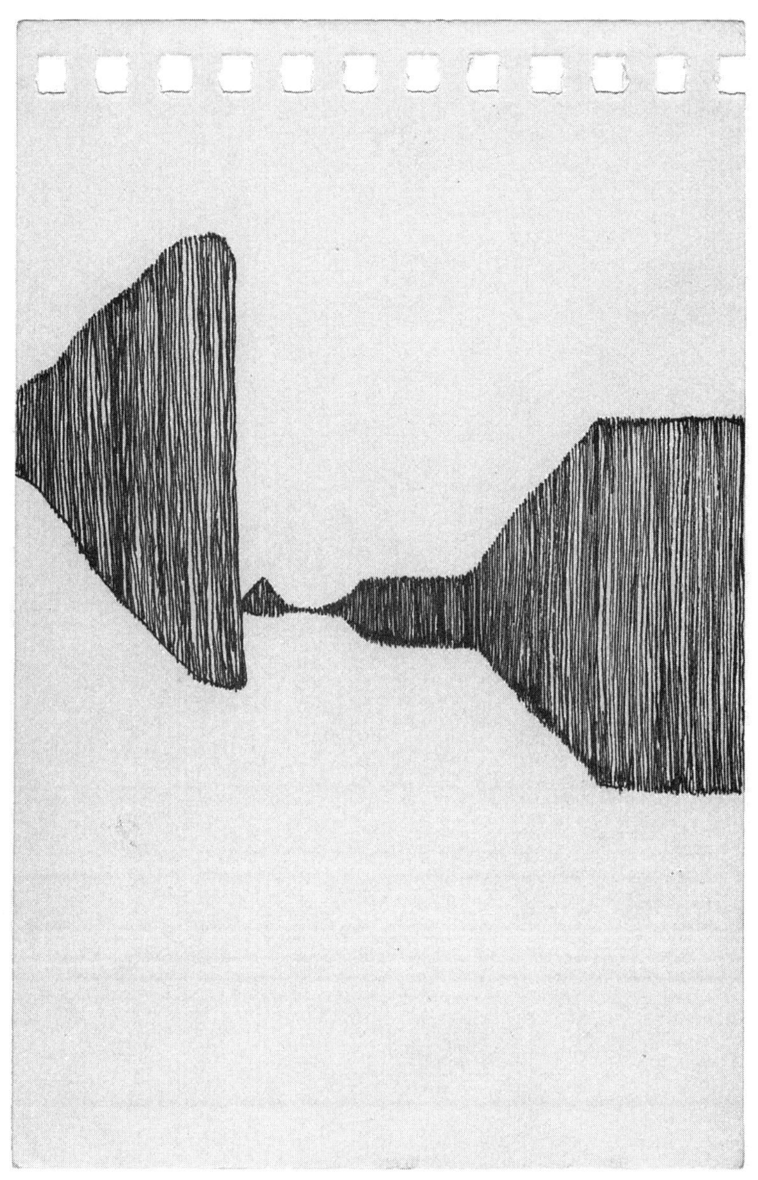

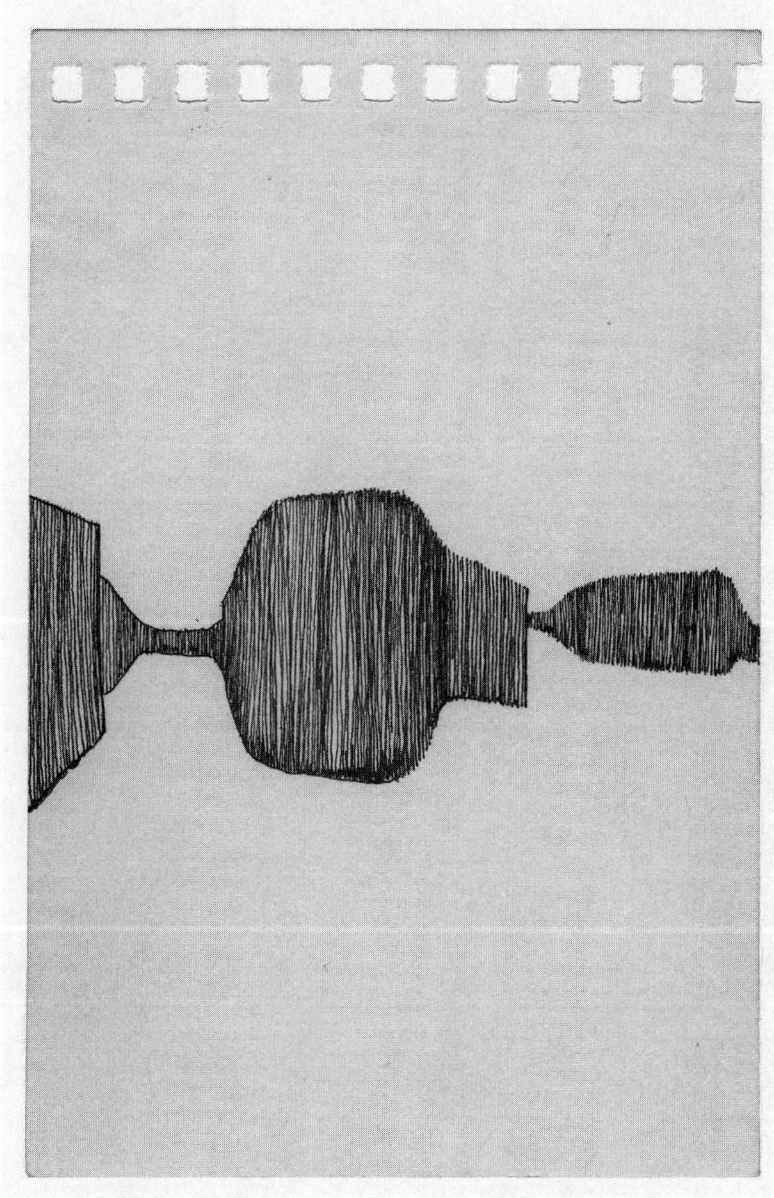

SLOPE

as against scatter

intermittent seismic

in Austria

graphite slides in

joints elide

recorded slopes

is it ecstasy

path and node

pattern arrival

binary code

networks

k is used

waves of elasticity

intercept form

at nexus note

not known why

sectors

as against stasis

Yearning to reorder the ontic things
pictures.
He reimages perceptual space,
between eye and stimuli,
entity provisionally thrown as delay.
Neurophysical seisms, infinite and organized
as draft environments.
Here each event as vector capturing slip, ripping.
He reimagines nervous graphs, physioscapes,
manifold braids of silence or fractured joy as continuous
functions that map the other in a correspondent fashion.
Burning to recreate living as photic.
Open, broken.
Tissue unknot so that each surface can reveal.
Yearning as order, both meter and differential,
he layers models by which the mechanics
of freeing tear retinal patterns, autonomous systems.
Image organize what *is* presents,
as environmental space in order to simplify
the theoretical slipping.
He strips breaks, measures discontinuities.
In these fragments futured arrivals.

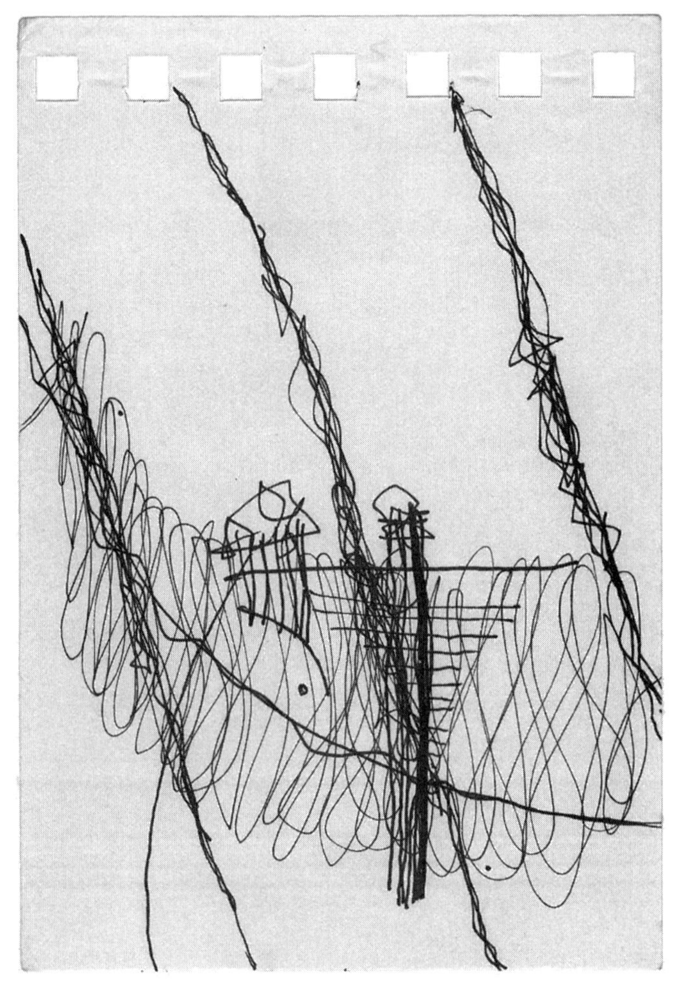

For a long time he drew regularly. He had drawn since he was small even before

Sensory, if I were to start in reflections and semblances, charting shadows and mirrored action. If I were to avoid descriptive. For example, this drawing does x, is

he spoke or wrote. His motivation for drawing was what it is for those who have no

y, or can be viewed as y, instead coming to stand within the visible. Is y? In the invisible, by extending the tension, avoiding metaphors as means or resorting to

sense of professionalism: an intimate act, his means of expression, a refuge, love.

numbers or proportion. Evading technique and echo. For example, explanation, though what are metaphors but stand-ins, conversations towards forms. The remainder

He loved to draw, to create in images worlds he could not live. After he ceased

As y, that is, to place them in the space of the work, in place, at sketch's edge. The text as an index of y, a reminder. True too of simile, seeing sameness or

to draw regularly he continued to—and sometimes still does—inhabit those secret

expressing it. Like y or its referent fields. As exegesis a mine and pitfall. Not to say, this is what this y means or reveals, or this is what it could tell if it were looked

regions to the detriment of real-world experiences and relationships. Perhaps he was not

into carefully, if we could say it and hold it there. Instead, I want to map about this feeling, the upheaval of falling for drawing, its spiritual and subordinate qualities, the

living enough in the present, in the now, for the day, today. Perhaps he was forestalling

process of seeing and mark-making. An interpretation though very likely not. If I were to pursue the text and observe the drawings then what would I think towards?

his current reality for some internal fantasy world he had realized only in his

Y and approximate feelings. The aim is balance. In a sense, then, I am writing independent of the drawing net, its wake or trace. In its margins, its absence as a way

drawings. It was real there but nowhere else (his interiority exteriorized), where his truths inhere.

of invoking it, not one but all of them, not all but specific amplitudes, these shifts, ethics. If I focus on sensory impression, as claim and wonder, asking why or how, a radical *now*.

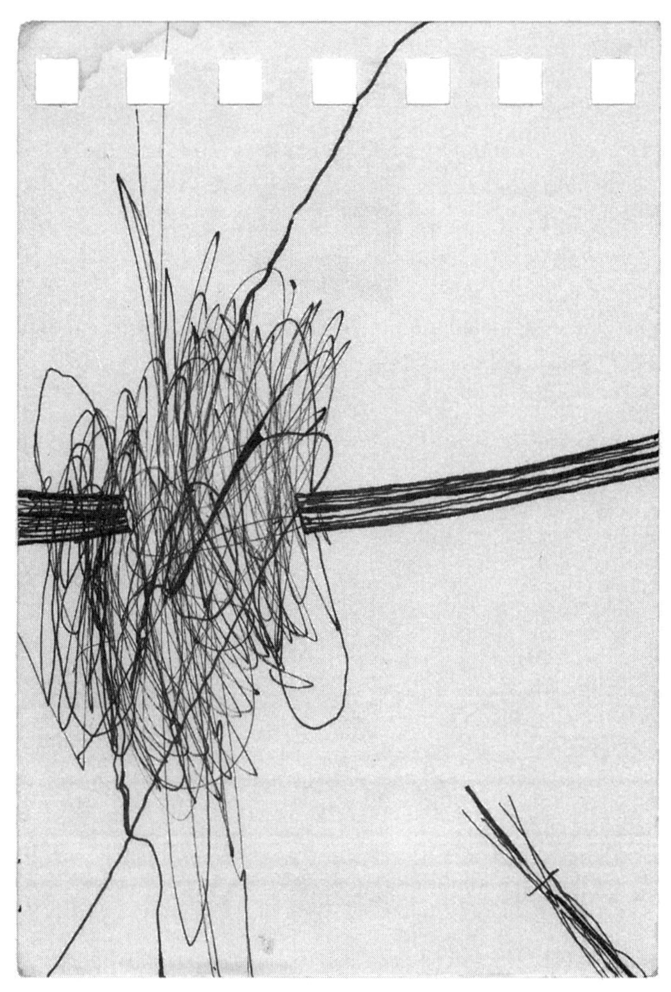

From many sources,
decomposition, blind
voices: vision. When searching
at the edge of self what is the source
of method, outside, the limit?
Driving at what is arriving,
you must parse it out.
Runs, parallels, a configuration
of plane, point, volume
relations: across
the initiatory continuum between
palm and performance,
desire stages: release
pleasure, draw it.
Highway of personal shadows
and yesterdays,
the intimate summoning
byway with its unfathomable brightness.
What does the image stammer
if you listen
carefully? Part of it is surprise,
reflects the terrifying
or sublime coming under, freeing as in
a mnemonic dissonance
or narrating others' forgotten
sexes, variables. Even tedium,
repetitive delirium. Parting,
so you empty and it becomes
yours—you. Another
is rigor that roils
about the idea
core. I—when I am others
inside myself,
eyes at the various
levels so I touch and embrace
new and luminous eruptions—

I—what we are deriving
from this graphite
facility, dark networks
of imaginaries that project
lyrical soul
color in each
squiggle, hatch?
From many sources, the signs
voicing clarity
and the risk of trying, the task
gathering action
inside: not complete,
till not mine, one mind
still in many
the limit hard
won, bearing ecstasy— not one
but many, undone:
redrawn: design

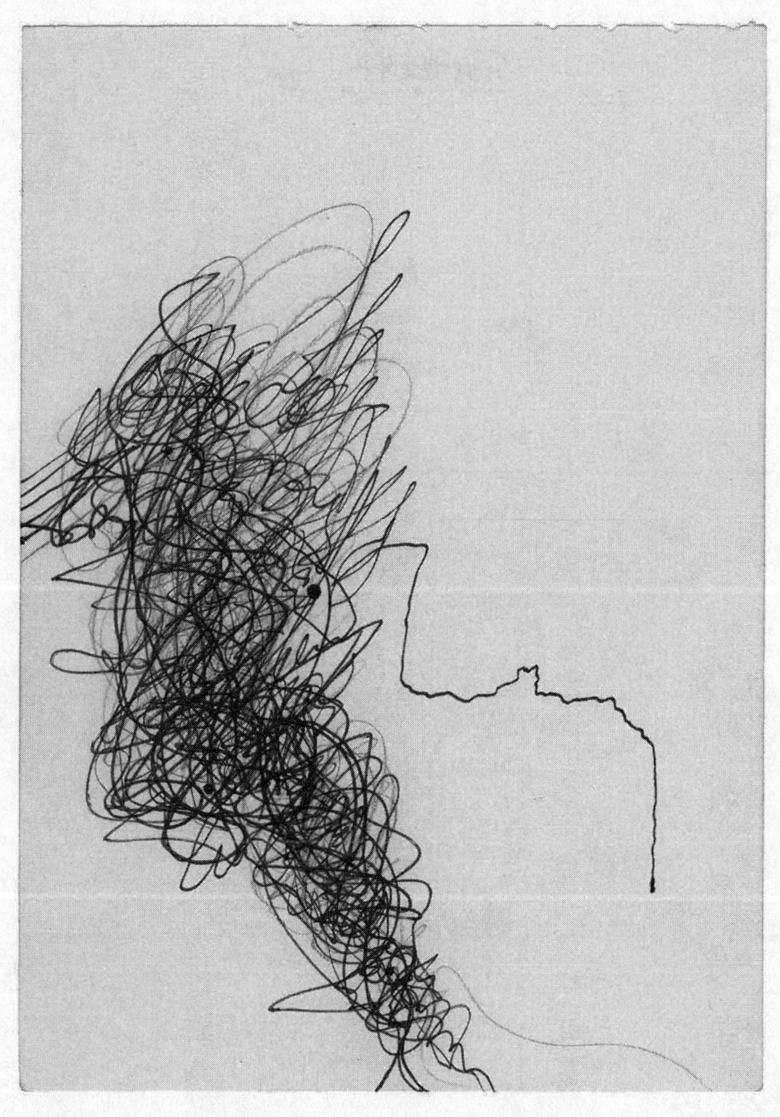

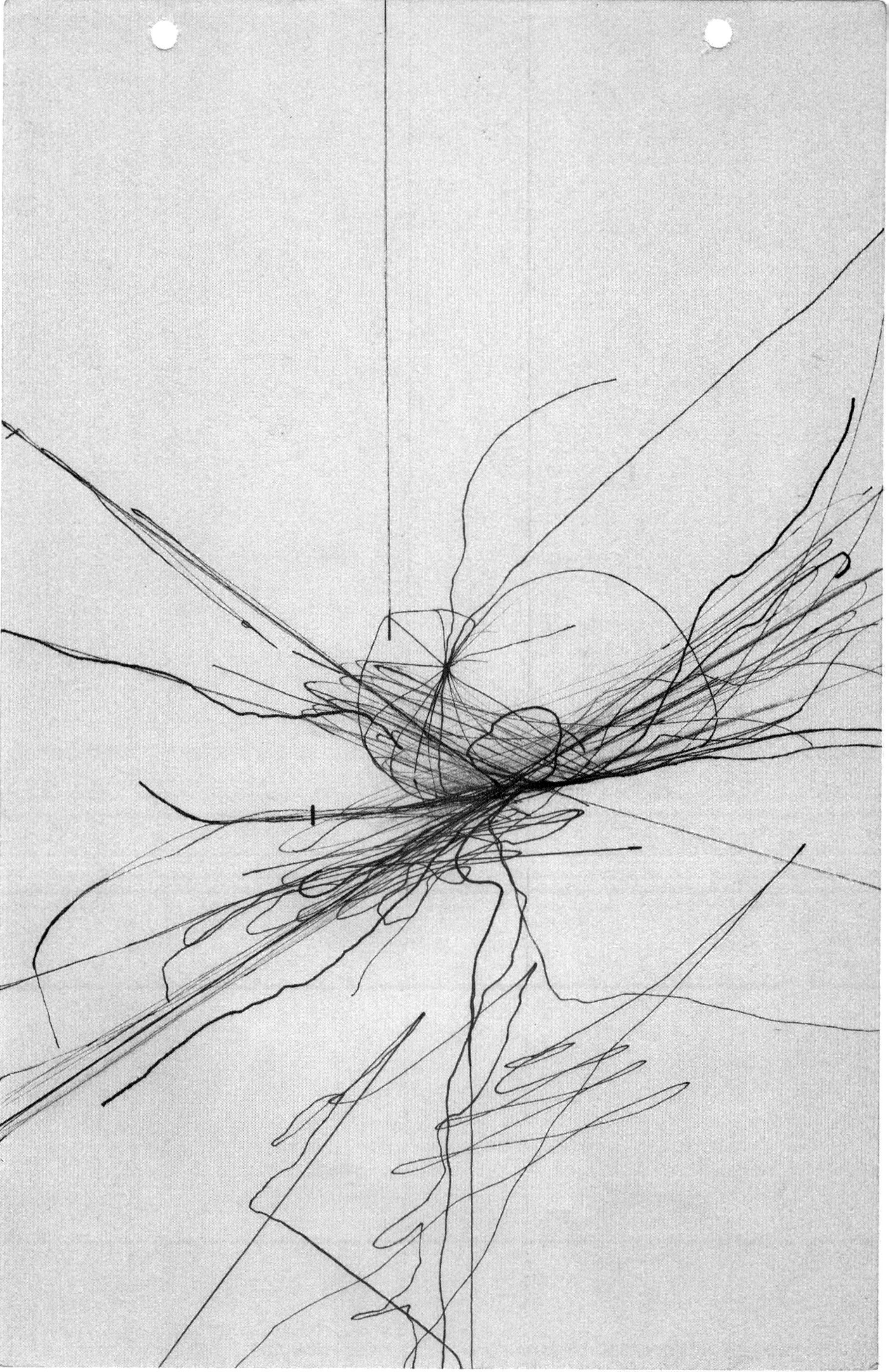

J: can't it be startling or referent perceptions surfacing
S: {transcription}

J: can't it be vision opened and reset by intimacy
S: {emotion}

J: can't it be modes viewed or renewed by familiar relation
S: {sublation}

J: can't it be manifold surface wave trajectory
S: {definition}

J: can't it be continual remapping of seismic shifts
S: {variation}

J: can't it be rotational value the eye computes as variable
S: {function}

J: can't it be cycling of the imagination's trajectory
S: {ritualization}

J: can't it be skills or fields intersecting at necessary angles
S: {information}

J: can't it be freeing measured in new neural pathways
S: {transformation}

AXIOMS

Following invisible axioms, struggling to translate them.

Image stalling on the threshold of echo

enigmatic signifier

Yet the axes are visible and return, this echo that grows, reveals its profoundest sense, what I strove to capture as a story of a vision (I once knew), an effortless music

of viewing

Now the tolling present pressing in, plaintive visions of chord and hinge (deeper)

What the singing connects and passes from string to finger or what lies, under

enigmatic signifier

Deeper, a rupture of retinal space, figure and surround, what was my station breaks

suspends

Suffering enters as figures, leaving their silvery trace, through darkness and flux the sound of dreamt disruption

of visional logic

Yet I strove through angles, emotion's topology or its distortion, how this pictorial vigor I swim in reroutes my circuit

enigmatic signifier

Layer on forms to page, as a study of game, parsing tropes or playing private shapes to public significance

Deeper still and yet superficial, rather than epic, this modest cycle alternately slack with underlap and a rigorous absence

that is always turning

What is visible: the sign enigma that punctures the tried idioms

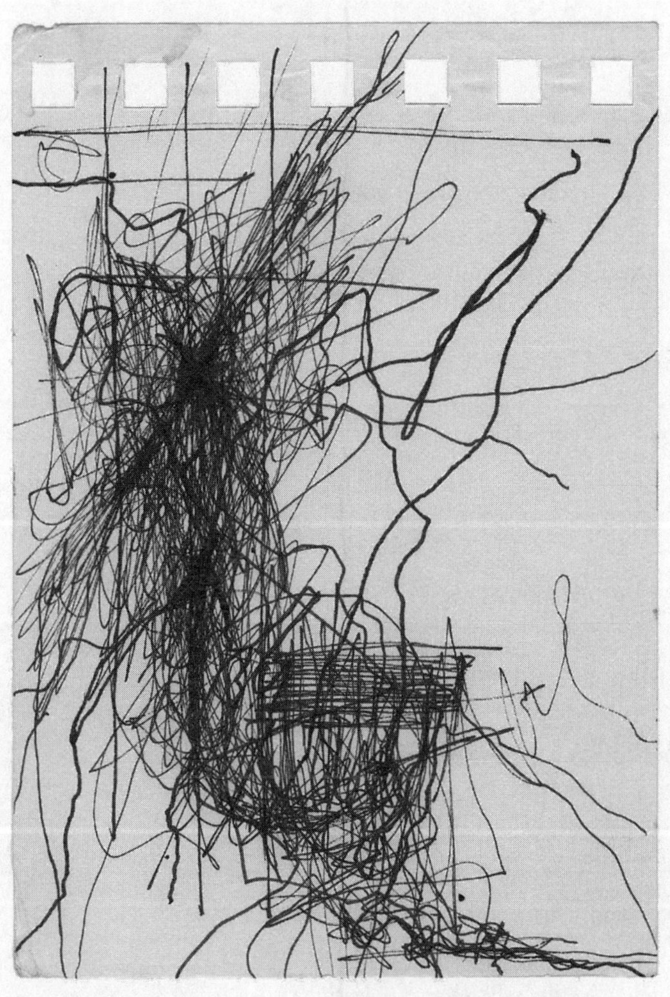

PERPENDICULAR

By talking through ourselves to our private margins

We are braking thinking, personal, introspective

We are linking exploratory, how to arrive at, embody lucid

We are drinking looking, or how to transcribe what eludes us

For our selves, or a chance to share and enter other ones

On sharing these, egos, eros and what slows us

By walking through this perpendicular of cloud sheave and stroke

We are leaving thinking, for expressive and physical intervals

We are layering thinking in intensity and its physical presentation

Graving in gesture the found and enfolding wave process

Breaking public messages, we who strive to form and respond

Making public modeling, rituals of the looking process

Within us transformations of structure, dynamics of impure story

Within us evolutions, reflecting wholes appropriating patterns

You, looking at thinking, uncoding referent mystery

We, deciphering hemisphere and plane we peer into, draw through

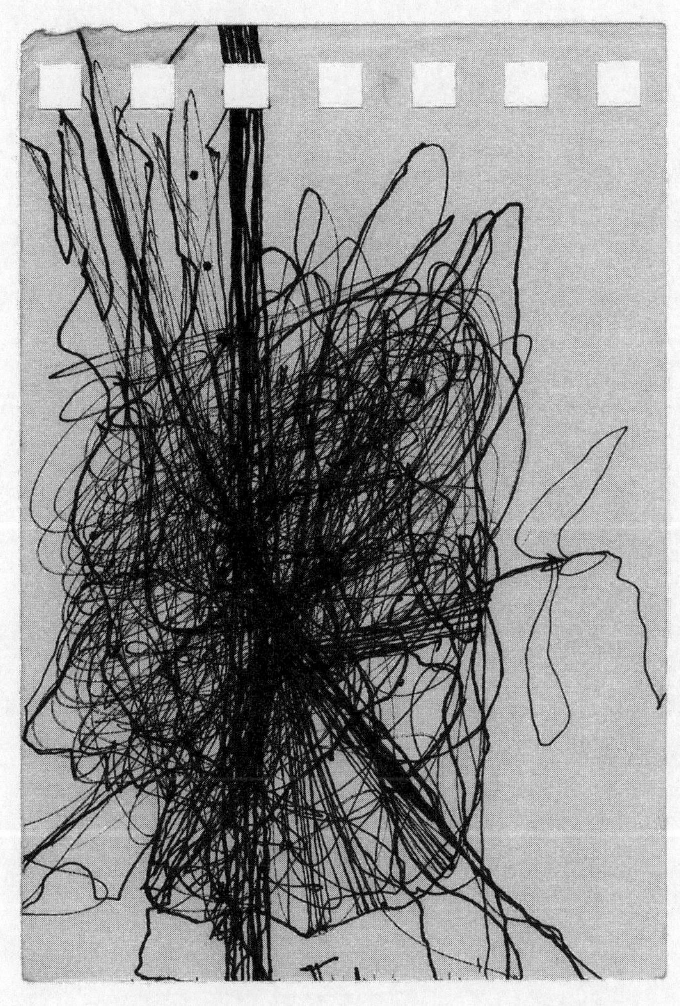

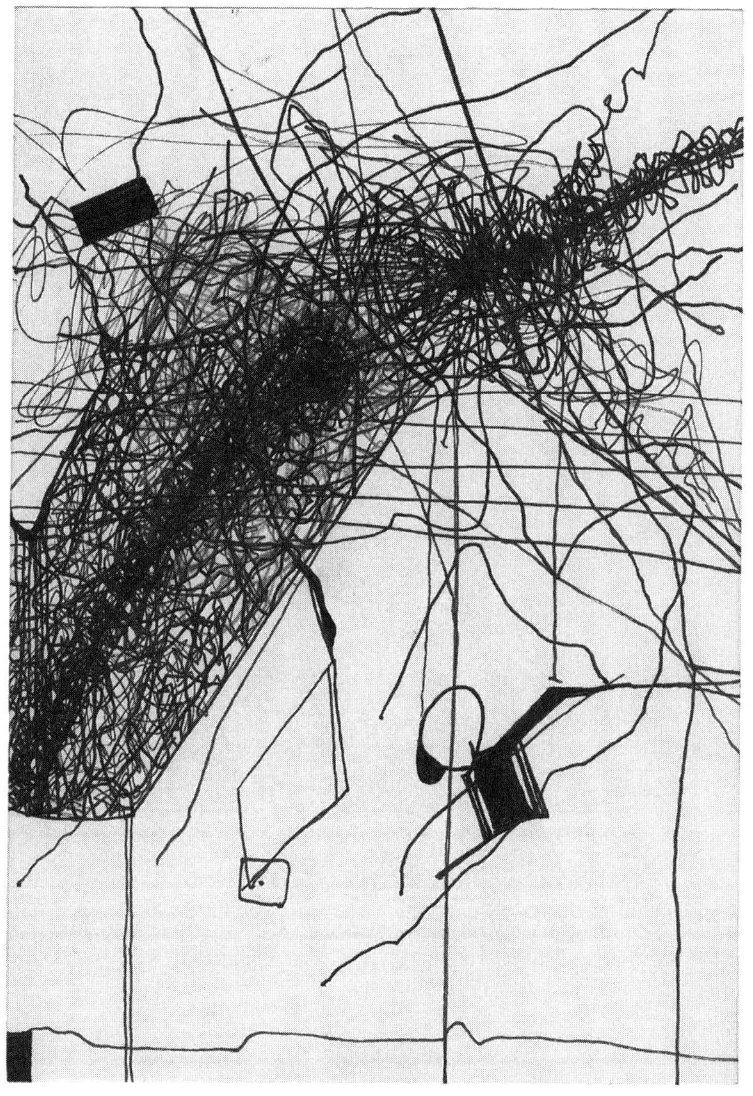

"through conceptualizing or drafting" *"mental"*

"statistical imagery" *"phantom"*
"articulated" *"information"*

"in denser fields" *"touches"*

"or at an angle" *"distilling"*
"pleasure" *"open"*

"desire structures" *"conceptual"*
"distilling" *"depth"*

"fantastical" *"draft"*
"private value" *"statistical"*

"and the blueprint may be true" *"angles"*
"reductive fictions" *"truly"*

"where distinct touch derives" *"conductive"*

"realizable phantoms" *"pictured"*
"or the mirror" *"denser"*

"not-yet-open" *"articulated"*
"pictorial turn" *"fields"*
"of minimal information" *"models"*

"gives concept" *"mirroring"*
"depth" *"value"*
"to original modeling" *"imaginaries"*

SURVEY

J: What is it that groups and readies itself?

J: What is veiled and always revealed?

J: Why is it heard and not only seen?

J: What is its economy of expression if we listen?

J: What lies behind the immediate, closer?

J: What is the feeling that passes through motion?

J: How is the vision broken, reconciled?

J: Within the narration where does the pictorial reside?

J: At what hour the pleasure of departure, the voyage?

J: Who communicates at the fault lines, the tremulous wholes?

J: What lies on the open, the distant side?

J: What is the probity in art, the honor?

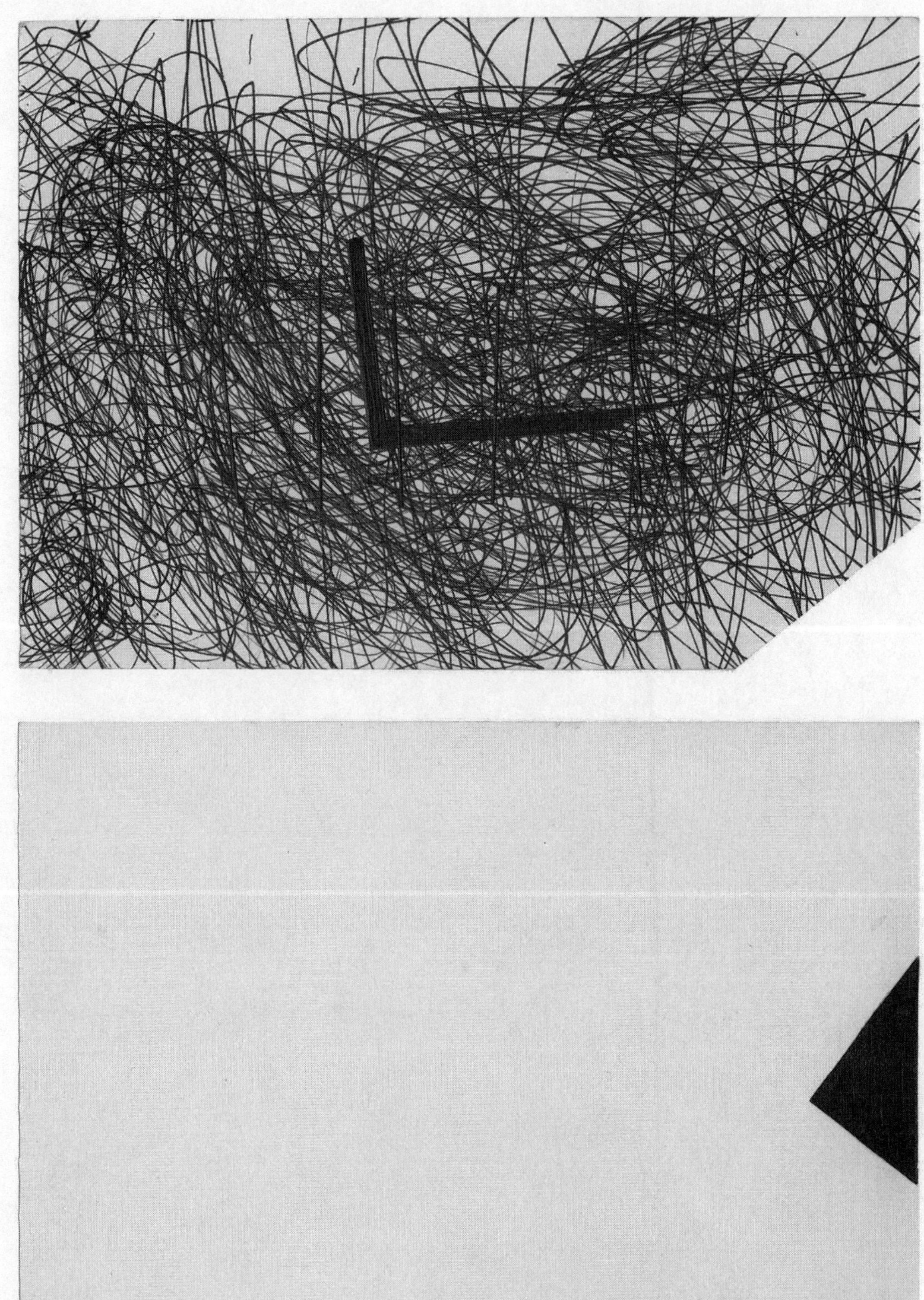

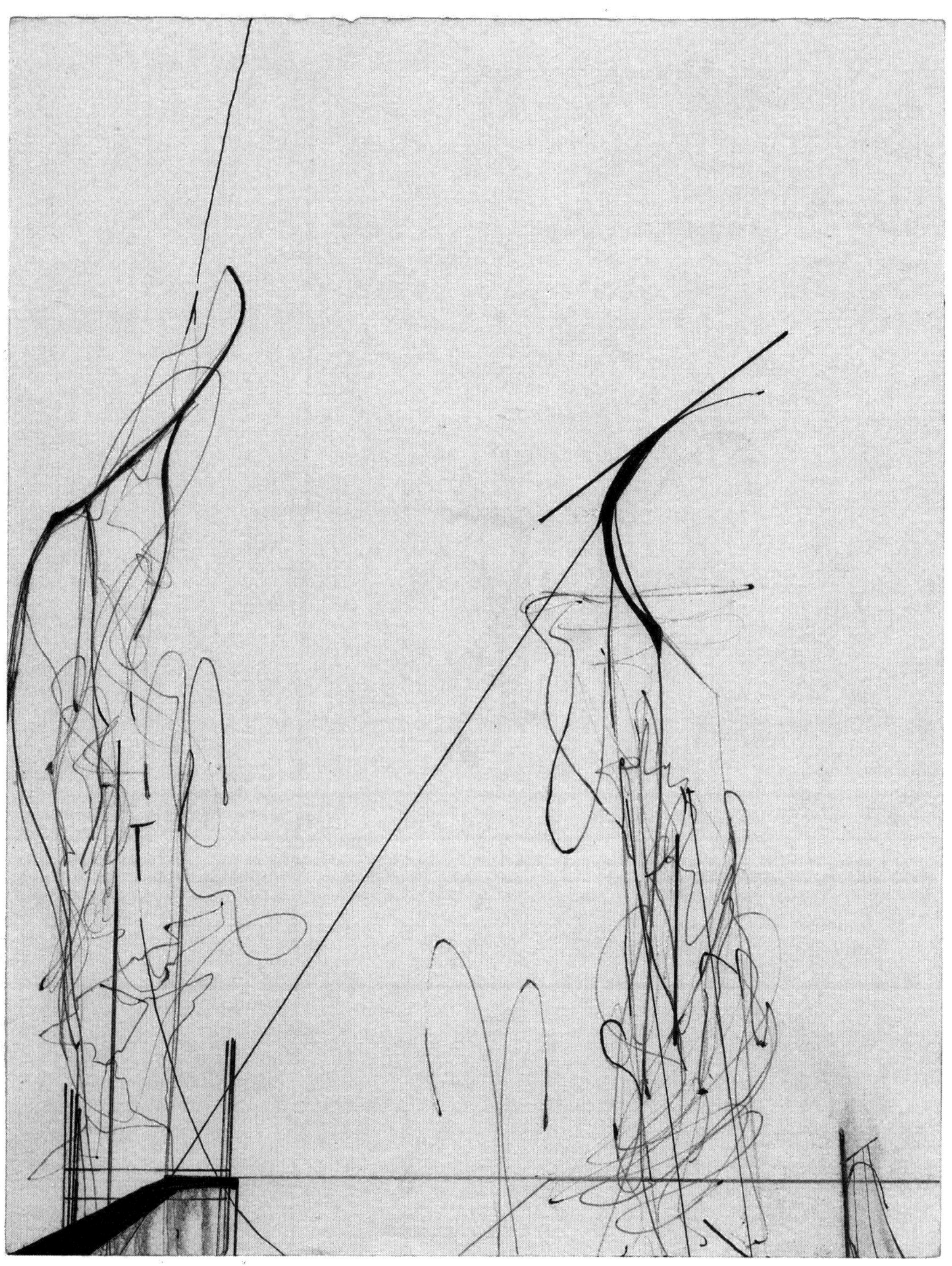

In the mark, we choose and lose signature.

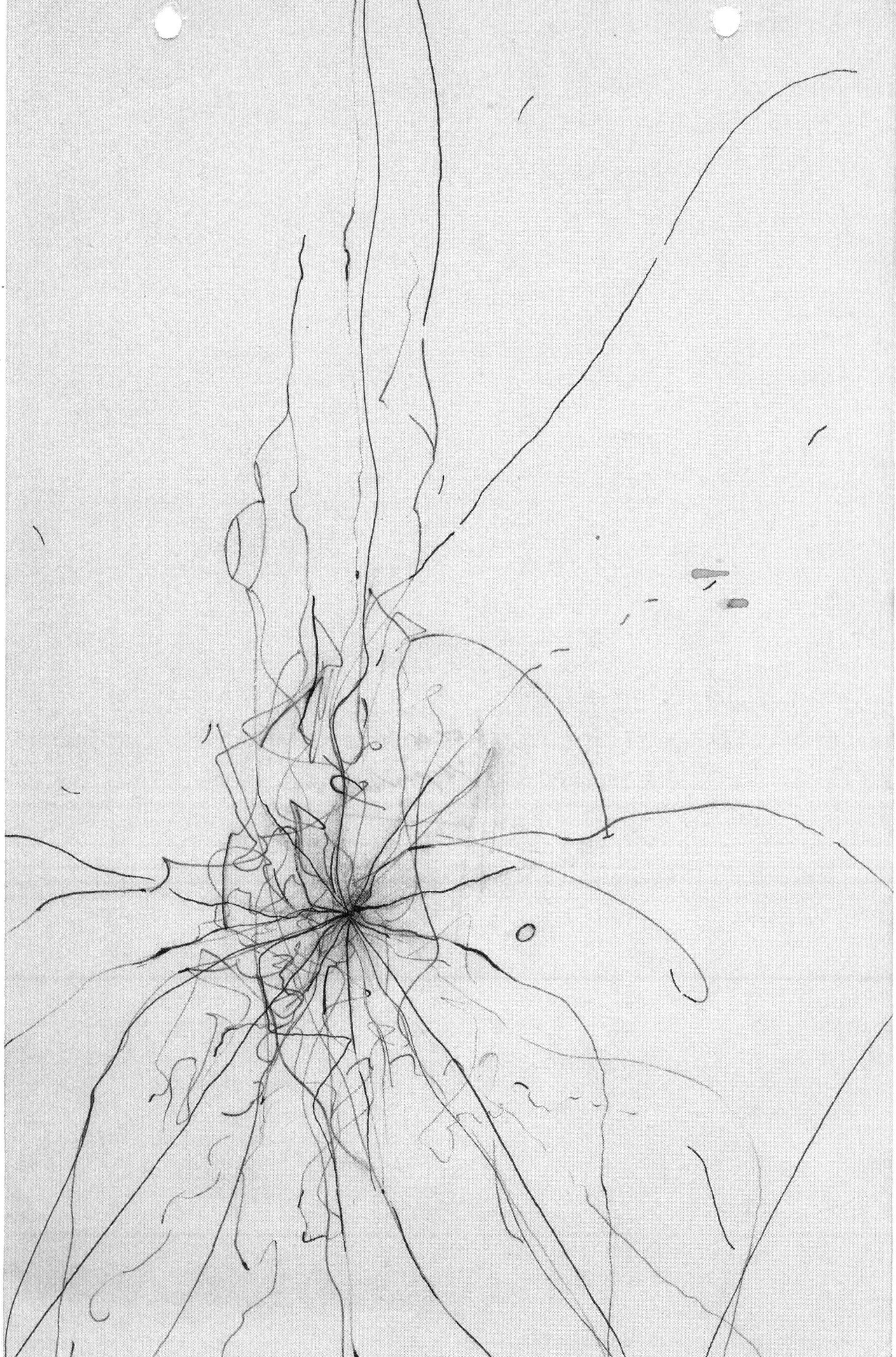

AFTERWORD

Geoffrey Jacques

With *Seismosis*, John Keene and Christopher Stackhouse give us a collection of texts and drawings that ranges in its deployment of language and image across a wide spectrum of contemporary reference. What is particularly appealing about *Seismosis* is the dense network of intertexuality that utilizes voice, image, and language as materials. Both texts and images serve as reflection upon—and communication with—each other, yet also as autonomous works in ways that reveal two unrelated, juxtaposed, yet simultaneously networked modes of presentation and expression.

My use of the terms "expression" and "voice" in describing Keene's texts is deliberate and, to some extent, intended as a formal provocation. This provocation involves features that may mark contemporary experimental verse practices conducted by African-American poets—namely, a refusal to disavow voice while paying close attention to the materiality of language:

among the Andeans clouds form

dynamics tile

opening like digital chrysanthemums

("After C(1): Anti-Mimesis")

In Keene's writing, both voice and language achieve a radical juxtaposition of metaphor ("dynamics tile" and "digital chrysanthemums") that remains a hallmark of language-based writing. At the same time, *Seismosis* sometimes contains an interplay of language and voice oddly reminiscent of Langston Hughes's work in the 1930s (I'm thinking of poems like "The Big Timer" and "Wait"). In Keene's "Membra," for instance, a group of phrases and words in quotes is arranged (in a form not unlike the “variable foot” of William Carlos Williams, or Ezra Pound’s stanza in the later Cantos) on the left side of a vertical line, while on the right, words—again in quotes—are arranged in sets of four, five, and six, moving down the vertical line. The stunning effect achieved here is not only a result of what appear to be randomly arranged quotes playing against each other—not only language “speaking” in the Heideggerian sense—it also appears that we are presented with a Utopia of plentitude, a polyvocal extravaganza whose center is at once everywhere and nowhere.

The claim I made earlier, that the *Seismosis* texts and images are both “unrelated” yet “networked” deserves further comment. Engaging this work, we witness collaboration in the densest meaning of the word. On the one hand, these are stand-alone texts and abstract drawings. On the other hand (and I’m thinking, now, of the spread whose text is “After C (2): Dialogue,” but you can choose just about any one of the spreads in the book), we come to see that each pair of texts and drawings can be read with—and against—each other. This is just the sort of networked collaboration one normally only comes across in poets who illustrate their own work. (Kenneth Patchen comes to mind, as do Vachel Lindsay, and Countee Cullen, who so beautifully illustrated his own book, *Copper Sun.*) In the case of two artists, this communication is typically unidirectional: the visual artist “illustrates” the poems (see the paintings Aaron Douglas made for *God’s Trombones* by James Weldon Johnson). In *Seismosis*, however, Keene and Stackhouse have attempted something utterly contemporary. The notion of the network (or the “rhizome,” after Gilles Deleuze and Felix Guattari) is very much at play in these interlacing texts and drawings. This polyform sort of collaboration between texts and images creates a textual environment where the groups of words themselves achieve a high level of abstraction, vis-à-vis the abstract drawings. Abstraction itself is destabilized in the decentered *Seismosis* field.

To return to my previous mention of Langston Hughes, in a critical attempt to deepen the provocation inherent in looking at—and reading—*Seismosis*, I would claim that the provocation here has to do with the “place” of this work within the precincts of experimental art making. There has yet to be a full accounting of the role African-Americans have played in the development of modernist and avant-garde literature. This is true despite the fact that black writers have been engaged in experimental poetic practices since before the birth of modernism. Even before the first stirrings of free verse and imagism in the early part of the last century—in such works as *Clotel* by William Wells Brown, with its aggressive use of pastische and found materials in the creation of narrative, and in the symbolist poetics of Paul Laurence Dunbar and William Stanley Braithwaite—black writers were engaged in the very practices that have been identified more readily with the avant-garde than with African-American writing. This lacuna ostensibly proves more problematic for literary criticism than for the writers themselves, yet Cary Nelson correctly notes that "we no longer know the history of the poetry of the first half of [the 20th] century." If this is true for poetry generally, it is doubly true—despite strenuous and largely successful efforts to counter this situation—for African-American writing.

This statement is also true of the visual arts. The aesthetic qualities of artists like Henry Ossawa Tanner and Jacob Lawrence are often pushed aside in favor of lavish attention paid their mythic or narrative qualities. Additionally, the history of black people's participation in the visual arts is encumbered by a historiography that is itself compromised by an identity steeped in complicity with the very processes of neglect and marginalization that make it difficult to gain a cogent understanding of the history of visual arts in the United States. For one thing, this complicity is tied up with a silence in regard to the relationship between design (in architecture, masonry, floor and wall tiles, clothing, and quilting) and the character of American-style abstract art making. Rozsika Parker and Griselda Pollock, for instance, demonstrate how the neglect of this relationship has led to the obfuscation of an understanding of the role of women in art history, and a serious look at the career of Lois Mailou Jones (to choose one example more-or-less at random) ought to raise serious questions about the way a blindness to these intersections has led to an ignorance regarding the history of abstract art making in the context of our own country's art history as a whole.

One symptom of the void I have just pointed to is the contentious and unsettled debate that persists within African-American critical and artistic circles, concerning the relationship between black writing and experimental poetics. The art term that embodies this problematic (perhaps more accurate to call it a term of critical categorization) is "Afro-Modernism." When faced with a work like *Seismosis*, such a term is and should be troubling. Earlier in this essay, I argued that one basic characteristic of the *Seismosis* drawings is their pure abstractness. A focus on "Afro-Modernism" diverts our attention from the roots that Stackhouse's drawings have in international practices of modern abstract image making. These images seem ready to burst from their frames, calling into play questions of space and time. But there are moments when one discerns hints of the recognizable, of the earth-bound. And here, again, is where the provocation I've been suggesting throughout this piece asserts itself .

The provocation is this: that among African-American artists who engage in experimental and avant-garde practices, there is a distinction that often leads to a kind of "identity trouble" (to slightly alter Judith Butler's famous phrase). The trouble is that black artists are concerned with the experimental, the edgy uses of elements that some may judge to be out of place within the precincts of such ("avant-garde") practices: the hint of the image within an abstract pictorial field, the use of voice within an otherwise language-based poetics. While some might argue that the use of such practices justifies worrying ourselves over the "relationship" between African-American artists, art, and the "avant-garde," one could just as easily, I believe, argue that such a worrying leads to an unnecessary narrowing of what constitutes avant-garde practice and the "tradition" of modernist and post-modernist artistic experimentation. And such worrying also leads us away from a productive reading of *Seismosis*—which, as a collection of texts, drawings, and their voices, is above all one that leads us into a world that both speaks and sings.

PUBLICATION ACKNOWLEDGEMENTS

Several of the poems appeared, in different versions, in the following literary journals, anthology, and in a limited edition artist book:

Four drawings from the "Perpendicular Series" appear in *Asemic Magazine.*

"Colors," "Prisms," and "*Sub Limine*" appear in *Aufgabe.*

"Love Waves," "Palimpsest," "Reflex," and "Sketchbook II / Intervals," as well as four of the "Perpendicular Series" drawings, appear in *Hambone.*

"Azimuth" and one of the "Perpendicular Series" drawings appear in *Indiana Review.*

"After C (3): Tayloriana," "Field," and "MO: Poesis" appear in *New American Writing.*

"Aura," "Field," "Klein Bottle," and "Prisms" were printed in letterpress type with 3 lithographic prints of drawings from the "Perpendicular Series" as "Seismosis," a limited edition artist book from the Center for the Book Arts, New York (2003).

"Oscillation," "Chamber Cinema," "Propositions," "Geodesy," "Reflex," "Prisms," "Map," "Love Waves," "Klein Bottle," "After C (2): Dialogue," "Fugues," "Slope," "Composition," and "Perpendicular," appear in *Inside the Outside: An Anthology of Avant-garde American Poets*, Roseanne Ritzema, editor, Rockford, Michigan: Presa Press (2006).

GENERAL ACKNOWLEDGEMENTS

The text samples words and texts by Kevin Bell, Yve-Alain Bois, Paul Brettell, Ernst Cassirer, Arthur Danto, Guy Davenport, Leonardo da Vinci, Robert Delaunay, Ulysse Dutoit, Briony Fer, Wassily Kandinsky, Daniel Libeskind, Colin McGill, Paul D. Miller/DJ Spooky, Barnett Newman, Mendi Lewis Obadike, Ogotommeli, Charles Olson, Marjorie Perloff, Adrian M. S. Piper, Richard Powell, Hanno Rempel, Robert Rindler, Jacques Roubaud, Christopher Stackhouse, Frank Stella, Cecil Taylor, and Rosmarie Waldrop.

John thanks Arthur Powell for his suggestions about exploring the mathematical field of topology, and in particular, about manifolds.

Our gratitude also to Il Panino Giusto and Doma, in New York City—where portions of this manuscript were discussed and written; and to Geoffrey Jacques and Ed Roberson for their words.

ABOUT THE ARTISTS

John Keene's poems, short stories, essays, reviews and translations have appeared in a wide array of periodicals and anthologies. A former member of the Dark Room Writers Collective and a graduate fellow of Cave Canem, he is author of *Annotations* (New Directions). Among his honors and awards are a 2003 Poetry Fellowship from the New Jersey State Council on the Arts and a 2005 Mrs. Giles Whiting Foundation Prize for fiction. He is an associate professor of English and African American Studies at Northwestern University.

Christopher Stackhouse's poems, drawings, and reviews on books, music, & art have been published in a range of art, literary, and entertainment publications. Stackhouse is an exhibiting artist with a focus in painting. His canvases and works on paper have been shown in New York City galleries including Wilmer Jennings Gallery and White Box: The Annex. He is the author of the poetry collection *Slip* (Corollary Press, 2005). Stackhouse is a Cave Canem Graduate Writer Fellow, a poetry editor at *Fence* magazine, and a 2005 Fellow in Poetry from The New York Foundation for the Arts.

1913
Press

www.1913press.org